ISAAC WATTS REMEMBERED

BY

DAVID G. FOUNTAIN

Published by
Mayflower Christian Bookshop
114 Spring Road, Bitterne, Southampton
SO19 2QB
also
Joshua Press, Burlington, Ontario, Canada

ISBN 0 903556 57 X

First published 1974
Second edition 1978
Third edition 1998

Printed and bound in Great Britain by
Itchen Printers Limited, Southampton

Cover design by Ruth Goodridge

FOREWORD

The great Dr. Johnson, orthodox of the orthodox, yet decided to include in his *Selection of English Poets* the works of Isaac Watts—a Dissenter—one of Southampton's most famous sons, and the writer of a larger number of hymns of the first rank than anyone except perhaps (and only perhaps) Charles Wesley—but still a Dissenter.

It is true that in his rather condescending *Life of Watts* Johnson wrote: "It is sufficient for Watts to have done better than others what no man has done so well." But he also wrote: "Happy will be that reader whose mind is disposed by his verses or his prose, to imitate him in all but his nonconformity, to copy his benevolence to man and his reverence to God. Few men have left behind such purity of character or such monuments of laborious piety."

In a letter to his publisher Dr. Johnson wrote: "To the *Collection of English Poets* I have recommended the volume of Dr. Watts to be added. His name has long been held by me in veneration."

For a Dissenter, in days of religious intolerance, to have made an impact on such a man as Dr. Johnson was indeed remarkable. As time has moved on "like an ever-rolling stream," that impact has spread throughout the English-speaking world. Of all hymns, "O God, our help in ages past" has become a precious part of the fabric of British life, and now especially associated with solemn national occasions, the greatest of them being the day on which we honour those who died in two world wars that Britain might remain a free country.

It is fitting that Southampton should honour this tercentenary of a great hymnwriter, a fearless son of an equally fearless Nonconformist father, one who loved children enough to write poems for them, and one whose life matched his preaching. Of him it could well be said, as of Chaucer's Poor Parson:

> "But Christ'es loore and His Apostles twelve
> He taughte, but first he folowed it himself."

And it is particularly appropriate that this new Life of Watts has been written by one in the long line of Dissenters, already author of an excellent account of the *Mayflower*, the Rev. David Fountain, M.A.

I count it a privilege to commend this book to all Southamptonians and the wider public.

Maybray-King.

I. WATTS. D.D.

CONTENTS

PREFACE TO THIRD EDITION

Since the first edition was written for the 300th anniversary of Isaac Watts birth in 1674 it became necessary to print a second one. This has just been exhausted so that a third edition is necessary. This is clearly providential since it coincides with the 250th anniversary celebrations of Isaac Watts death in 1748.

The only difference to the new edition is that it has a new front cover which is the work of Ruth Goodridge for which we are very thankful. We also remain thankful to Southampton City Council Cultural Services Division for the supply of photographs throughout the book and to Michael Underwood for the line drawings.

As a further part of the 250th celebrations the publisher has produced a selection of 50 Hymns from Watts "Hymns and Spiritual Songs". The first of these was written specifically for the Southampton congregations where his father was a deacon.

D.G.F.

INTRODUCTION

Ten years ago I purchased the complete works of Isaac Watts, in six beautifully bound volumes, for the sum of twenty-five shillings. At the same time I obtained Milner's "Life and Times of Watts" at a very reasonable price. I had been interested in Watts before, since he is such an outstanding Southampton figure, but I was now armed with the means of discovering more about him. On one occasion I was singing a hymn of Isaac Watts's and noticed the dates of his life that followed his name at the bottom of the hymn. It then occurred to me that we would be remembering his birth in 1974. Having written a book on the story of the Mayflower pilgrims, which story was closely associated with Southampton, I naturally desired to produce something that would remind us of him.

The name Isaac Watts is known the world over. I believed it could be of service and help to many if they knew something about the man who had written such wonderful hymns. My aim in writing this book is to provide the knowledge of this great poet that will enable those who sing his hymns to appreciate them more.

About four years ago I informed Basil Henning, of the Entertainments and Publicity Department, of my intention to write this volume. I was delighted when, later, I was asked if I would wish it to be made an official part of the Southampton celebrations of the 300th Anniversary of Watts' birth. I was further delighted when Lord Maybray King, former Speaker of the House of Commons, consented to write a Foreword. He seemed the most obvious person to represent the City in this way, being the most eminent of our citizens, and in other ways specially suited to being associated with Isaac Watts. His own contribution to education, particularly his association with Richard Taunton's College (with which Watts was indirectly connected), his appreciation of Isaac Watts' hymns, and his own position as a Dissenter qualify him in a particular way to write the Foreword. In it he quotes from Chaucer's Prologue, and there is good reason to believe that the Poor Parson was one of Wycliffe's Lollards—the first English Dissenters!

It is my hope and prayer that this memorial to one who was the gift of God to the Church will not only be of interest, but will help us to appreciate the legacy that he has left us, to the glory of God.

March 1974, Southampton. David G. Fountain

Early Years in Southampton: 1674–1685 (up to 11 years)

Chapter 1

It is the year 1674; the place is God's House Tower, Southampton.[1] A woman sits on a horse-block outside the prison, nursing her child. It is a hard seat, but not so hard as the hearts of her husband's persecutors, for he is inside, imprisoned for refusing to conform to the laws of the land relating to the worship of God. He is prepared to pay the price, as he would rather serve God than man, for he believes that Scripture alone should be our guide in worship.

He and his wife had been married but a year, and although he could not see the child's face, the sound of his crying would give him pleasure. How much more pleasure it gave him in later years when that child, who was born so small and sickly, was to influence the worship of the nation more than any other single man. The father, indeed, was suffering for his convictions regarding the worship of God, and those convictions were conveyed to his son, but his son, Isaac, had the opportunity and ability to give expression to them to an unimaginable degree. Isaac Watts became the father of the English Hymn, and the writer of more hymns in popular use than any other man, except possibly Wesley. The impact of his father's faith never left the son, and the son gave it an expression which has enriched the worship of Christians throughout the world ever since.

What kind of a man was Isaac Watts? We can form some idea from an essay written after a violent thunderstorm in which he wrote the following words: "Happy the soul whose hope in God composes all his passions amid these storms of nature, and renders his whole deportment peaceful and serene amid the frights of weak spirits and unfortified minds." Here and elsewhere Watts speaks of the importance of remaining calm and even cheerful amidst the trials of life. He himself succeeded in doing this to a large degree, for while his outward circumstances were generally very comfortable, he was frequently ill. However, he remained unruffled, but this was not due to his nature for he was, we are told, 'passionate and waspish,' but due to his confidence in the goodness of God. He was able to apply to himself the 'soothing oils' which he constantly recommended to his readers, many of whom were in circumstances altogether different from his, and frequently suffering persecutions of various kinds for their faith. Watts, however, was not to be distinguished only as a man who could bear much hardship cheerfully. This was but the background to a life of constant activity in which he sought by every means in his power to further the kingdom of God. He was aware of the fact that he had been given many advantages and was determined to use them to the glory of the One to whom he owed all things. Every skill and every opportunity was used to its fullest, to the single end of serving his master, the Lord Jesus Christ, to the benefit of His church on earth. He worked so hard, and for such long hours, however, that he had cause to regret it in later life. Thus, Watts was both content to bear his lot and use the gifts God had given him to the full.

Let us begin our story by tracing some of Isaac Watts's ancestors. His grandfather, Thomas Watts, was a remarkable man. He commanded a warship in the year 1656 and his personal courage was outstanding. On one occasion while in the East Indies he was pursued by a tiger into a river and turned to grapple with the animal and, by his coolness and skill, succeeded in driving off the beast. In the war with the Dutch the vessel he commanded exploded, and by this accident he was killed in the prime of life. He was no rough seaman but good at mathematics, music, painting and poetry. His grandson, Isaac, wrote these words in his memory:

"Since he was seen on earth no more:
He fought on lower seas and drown'd;
But victory and peace he found
On the superior shore."

The poem from which the above lines are taken was dedicated to Isaac Watts' grandmother. She survived her husband for some time and almost saw her grandson finish his studies for the Christian ministry. The composition showed how much he thought of her. In his early education she played an important part, and sought to have a godly influence upon him. In his ode after her death he follows his 'revered preceptress' to her 'celestial dwelling,' and in the character which he assumes, that of a 'painter-muse,' thus pictures her spirit:

> "I know the kindred mind. 'Tis she, 'tis she;
> Among the heavenly forms I see,
> The kindred mind from fleshly bondage free;
> O how unlike the thing was lately seen
> Groaning and panting on the bed,
> With ghastly air, and languish'd head,
> Life on this side, there the dead,
> While the delaying flesh lay shivering between!"

Isaac Watts's father (also named Isaac), received a classical education and, like his more gifted son, had a passion for poetry and a taste for art.

When, in 1662, the "Act of Uniformity" was passed, and two thousand ministers were ejected from the Church of England, two Southampton ministers were among them: Nathaniel Robinson, the Rector of All Saints, and Giles Say, the Vicar of St. Michael's. Non-conformity had begun in the neighbourhood. Robinson was "affectionately encircled by a few who entreated him to be their minister." The worshippers met secretly in various houses, but most frequently in a tenement just behind the Bargate, which afterwards became the property of Isaac Watts the elder. The pastor of this group was Nathaniel Robinson. Giles Say gathered his company at first secretly, and then afterwards in his own house in Blue Anchor Lane. Isaac Watts, senior, became a member of Robinson's 'Independent' church and, subsequently, a Deacon.

Southampton at this time was very different from the place it now is. Its population was only a few thousand. It was, we are told, "a charming little sequestered town, the gentle river (Itchen) rolled its pleasant and lucid waves before it, undisturbed by the iron floating bridge, and unsullied by steamboats,"[(2)] but this is a misleading picture. In 1665 the town had been nearly depopulated by the Plague. The richer inhabitants fled in panic. Those left behind could not bear the burdens that fell on so small a company. The shops shut, and the deserted streets became entirely overgrown with grass. Famine threatened the poor who remained. Thirty years later, in 1695, it was still in a low state. It was reported that it was "not in the same flourishing state as formerly for, having lost its trade it has also lost most of its inhabitants, and the great houses of its merchants are now dropping to the ground and only show its ancient magnificence." After the turn of the century it was reported again that the population was so small that the five churches were more than adequate for the inhabitants. Further comment speaks of the town as "an old fortification run to ruin," and that "the trade of the town is inconsiderable, and the vessels that lie here are but few."

Persecution

The town, we know, was the scene of persecution, but so were many other places at this time. Let us look for a moment, therefore, at life among the Dissenters at this period, for Isaac Watts, senior, was not alone in his suffering. It has been said that the period from 1662 to 1688, the year of the "glorious revolution," when William of Orange replaced James II as King of England, was the "golden age of Independency." Though it was a period of intense persecution the "Independent" churches flourished. These particular churches were described thus because they were each self-governing communities. The persecution was widespread but varied immensely in its intensity. It was never systematic over the whole period nor over the whole country. However, Nonconformists (i.e. Independents, Baptists, Quakers and Presbyterians) were under constant threat of having their meetings broken up and of being fined. They needed great patience, and responded, through the grace of God. It was a period when those ministers who were unable to preach used the opportunity to write. The Puritan ministers whose names are famous, such as Owen, Goodwin and Manton, published their works at this time, and John Bunyan wrote most of his works at this period. "Pilgrim's Progress" appeared in 1678. The ejected ministers, like Robinson and Say, were mostly men of learning and suffered considerably. Few of them were permitted to earn a reasonable wage. In spite of hardship the congregations increased up and down the country. Independent churches outside the Church of England were joined by those that had been formed within the parochial system and were driven out in 1662. The established Church and Government felt threatened as they saw the growing numbers of Dissenters. They feared that Cromwellian forces would once again challenge their power! It was not many years since the Church of England had been replaced by the Presbyterians as the Established Church. Scandalous rumours about the intentions of Nonconformists were spread and punitive Acts of Parliament were passed. However, the people themselves did not share the zest for harassing Nonconformists, especially after the established ministers chose to desert their posts in London during the Plague of 1665, when the ejected ministers took the opportunity to fill vacant pulpits. To the majority, the Plague and the burning of a sizeable part of London in '66 were regarded as a 'Divine visitation.'

Suppression

The authorities were not to be dissuaded. In 1670 a Bill was introduced which was described as "the quintessence of arbitrary malice." It was described as an Act "to prevent and suppress seditious conventicles." The malicious aspect of this Bill lay not only in the heavy fines, but in the fact that the sworn evidence of two informers was sufficient to gain prosecution, and that these informers themselves were given a third of the fine! A survey was carried out by the established Church as to the extent of Nonconformity. The results alarmed them as to its widespread character. Dr. John Owen stood out as the leader of the Nonconformists. (Isaac Watts occupied his pulpit in later years, and for this and other reasons Owen's mantle fell on him.) In 1672 relief was granted to the Dissenters at the 'Declaration of Indulgence.' Upon this event, the Dissenters in Southampton met for worship in Mr. Say's house, which was licensed at Whitehall on the 2nd May. "We do hereby permit and license Gyles Say of the congregationall persuasion, to be a teacher of the congregation allowed by us in a Roome or Roomes, in his House, in Southampton, for the use of such as do not conform to the Church of England, who are of the persuasion commonly called Congregationall."(3) In 1673, however, the Declaration was revoked. Say and Watts were thrown into Southampton gaol (God's House Tower) for refusing to conform. In the elder Watts' poems there are several references to his 'darksome, melancholy cell.' These were strange days. Immorality was open and moral standards appalling. A man might 'swear like a Briton' and be 'as drunk as a Londoner,' but if he chose to say his prayers in his own way he was a menace to society and guilty of a criminal offence!

Freed

Watts was out of prison by 11th September, 1673, for on that day he married Sarah Taunton, daughter of Mr. Alderman Taunton, a pious woman and a woman of taste. Her father was descended from the Huguenots who escaped from France to England after the massacre of Protestants in Paris on St. Bartholomew's Day, 1573. A community of Huguenots flourished in the town. One of his grandchildren, Richard Taunton, founded Taunton's College in 1760. Watts settled in 41, French Street,(4) where he conducted a boarding school of such repute that pupils from America and the West Indies were committed to his care. Apparently the persecution to which he was subjected ruined his academy. We are told he was 'a clothier,' i.e. clothmaker. This may well have been his trade before he had to give up his school, for many dissenters learnt a trade and combined it with teaching and preaching. His mother and his wife's parents lived nearby. The young couple were constantly harrassed by their enemies and Watts was again imprisoned. The strain on his wife was considerable, and when their first child, Isaac, was born on 17th July, 1674, he was small and sickly. He was baptised about September, the actual date not being recorded "by reason of an unsetled estate of the church att the tyme." The elder Watts had as his constant companion in his cell a pocket Bible in which he wrote, "Teach me to understand aright Thy sacred Word, and with delight shall I peruse it day and night." He was released in the following year and able to rejoin his family and give Isaac that precious instruction which made so much of an impact on his sensitive nature.

Isaac Watts, junior, was a good pupil. Even when he was very young he showed a remarkable passion for learning. When he was given money he would run to his mother crying, "A book, a book; buy me a book!" One can imagine the Watts family (for there were seven other children besides Isaac), in the old house in French Street. They would gather in the large kitchen; the cheerful fire would light up the blue Dutch Scriptural tiles which decorated the hearth of 'Puritan' homes. The children would be dressed as their parents were, as was the custom in those days. After the meal, the father would read from the large family Bible. On the fly-leaf of this Bible a list of their children, besides Isaac, is found. The names of Richard, Enoch, Thomas, Sarah, Mary—and a second Mary (the first lived only two years)—and Elizabeth are entered. Elizabeth also died after two years. After the reading of a chapter from this Bible, he used to engage in prayer. He would never allow himself to be disturbed in his devotions, for if, while he was upon his knees, any one called to see him, the servant was sent out with the message, "My master is at prayer." The remainder of the day was devoted chiefly to the instruction of his pupils. It was during family prayers on one occasion that Isaac the younger showed his poetic skill. While they were at prayer Isaac was heard to titter. His father demanded the cause of his merriment. "Because," he replied, pointing to the bell-rope by the fireplace, "I saw a mouse run up that and the thought came into my mind

> 'There was a mouse, for want of stairs,
> Ran up a rope to say his prayers."

This early disclosure of his ability was encouraged by his parents, and when his mother offered a reward of a farthing to those of her husband's pupils who could compose the best lines, Isaac tried and produced this couplet:

> "I write not this for a farthing, but to try
> How I your farthing writers can outvie'."

Isaac had a close attachment to his parents, and when he later went away to London he felt this loss of their company.

In 1680, when he was 6, the great comet of that year was the marvel and wonder of the day. Watts frequently spoke in after life of the deep impression that this brilliant wanderer made upon his youthful mind. It doubtless contributed to the interest he developed in astronomy.

Education

He received his earliest education from his father including the study of Latin at 4 years of age. When he was 6 he was sent to the 'Free School' then situated in Winkle Street. (This later became known as King Edward VI Grammar School.) Here he was under the care of Rev. John Pinhorne, Rector of All Saints. He became very warmly attached to Mr. Pinhorne, and addressed some verses to him. His mother gave him much of her time, and was careful to teach him from the Scriptures. His parents were thrifty, and this habit evidently remained with Isaac, since he was careful to secure a good financial return for his many literary labours!

Before Isaac Watts was six he composed some verses. When they fell into the hands of his mother, she doubted that he really wrote them. To satisfy her as to his ability to compose in this manner, he penned the following acrostic upon his name:

"I am a vile polluted lump of earth,
S o I've continu'd ever since my birth;
A lthough Jehovah grace does daily give me,
A s sure this monster Satan will deceive me,
C ome, therefore, Lord, from Satan's claws relieve me.
"W ash me in thy blood, O Christ,
A nd grace divine impart,
T hen search and try the corners of my heart,
T hat I in all things may be fit to do
S ervice to thee, and sing thy praises too."

The events of this part of his life are thus recorded by him in his memoranda:

"Coincidents.	Memoranda.	
	Began to learn Latin of my father	1678.
	To Latin school and writing	1680.
1683 My father persecuted and imprisoned for nonconformity six months. After that forced to leave his family and live privately in London for two years.	Began to learn Greek ..	1683 or before.
	I had ye small pox ..	1683.
	Learnt French	1684, 1685.
	Learnt Hebrew	1687 or 8."

In the year of Mr. Watts's imprisonment, the persecution of the protestant dissenters was at its height. It is impossible to form a correct estimate of the sufferings of the nonconformists at this time; much has been written to minimise their distress, but the record of the acts of parliament speaks for itself. Those who failed to attend church on Sundays were liable to the censures of the church, and fined 1s. for each offence, £20 per month for continual personal absence, and £10 per month for the non-attendance of their servants. These fines were recoverable by the seizure of land, and penalties included imprisonment and exile. Those who were once banished and returned faced death. Ministers of the protestant dissenters were by the Act of Uniformity subject to a penalty of £100 for administering the Lord's supper; by the Five-mile Act were prohibited under a penalty of £40 from coming within five miles of any city, town corporate, or borough; and by the Conventicle Act they forfeited £20 for the first offence, and for the second offence, £40, if they preached in any place "at which there should be five or more besides those of the household."

Lest anyone should be bored with these details let them consider the fact that there are some striking similarities between the sufferings of the 17th century English Nonconformists and the 20th century Russian "dissenters."[5]

One of Isaac Watts's well-known hymns well expresses the attitude of those who faced such persecution:

"I'm not ashamed to own my Lord,
Or to defend His cause;
Maintain the honour of His Word,
The glory of His cross."

(Hymn No. 19 Appendix V)

The hardest period for the Nonconformists was during the 80's. Even so, in many areas there were so many of them, and some were so influential, that it was very difficult for the authorities to enforce the Act. They were obliged even to fine magistrates for refusing to carry out the law and stop the loopholes of which they made use! Although the death penalty had not been legally prescribed, many suffered death through disease and undernourishment in filthy prisons. It is estimated that no less than 15% of the Nonconformists suffered at some time from imprisonment. But the levying of fines was more damaging. There was some justification for the exaggerated statement of the Yarmouth people that 'the Nonconformists were paying the best part of the nation's costs.' The congregations stood firm with their ministers and many ingenious devices were used to avoid informers and consequent prosecution! In London, meetings were held in densely-populated alleys. One Government spy reported: "By reason of so many back doors, bye-holes and passages, and the sectarians so swarming thereabouts, I have been afraid of being discovered in scouting." At Yarmouth an informer was impressed by the conventicle held there. One Sunday in June, 1668, he kept it under observation throughout the day and reported that the morning meeting lasted from between 5 and 6 in the morning until 10, and the next service from 11 until 3 in the afternoon, during which time he counted no less than 400 leaving the meeting through the one door he watched![6]

Thomas Jollie at Windmond House had a door, which led from the meeting-house to a staircase, cut in two. He stood on the stair case behind the door to preach, while the top of the door, fitted on hinges, served as his desk. A string was conveniently attached to this makeshift desk so that all he had to do when he was given a warning was to pull the string so that the top half of the door closed. When the informers came in they would find a congregation but no preacher! Meetings were held in the open air, woods, caves and even on rocks out at sea at low water. Some fine meeting places were built, nevertheless. The congregations were divided into those who were "members" and under the discipline of the church, and a larger number described as "hearers" (regular members of the congregation). Joseph Caryl's London church, for instance, had 136 members in 1673, when it merged with Owen's church (the congregation over which Watts later presided) but the census of 1669 suggested that 500 attended Caryl's 'conventicle.' The churches were very close-knit, and had the character of a spiritual family. Though they maintained a strict separation from the Church of England many were willing to attend the ministry of men they respected, and practised occasional Communion in the Church of England in order to qualify for public offices. Expository preaching from Scripture occupied a large proportion of the services. It was careful, scholarly, doctrinal and lengthy, and "it came home to conscience and had the greatest tendency to do good." People who came together at some risk would not be content with sermonettes. Free prayer accompanied the preaching of the Word of God. The hymn-singing, however, left much to be desired, as we shall see later. These points are of interest when we remember that the Above Bar congregation in Southampton was a typical 'Independent' church.

Watts wrote his hymns for the whole Christian world, but especially for the congregation he was most familiar with. This was only natural. We conclude this chapter with one of his hymns that was particularly suited to the dissenting congregation. As with so many of Watts's hymns it is based on Scripture.

"We are a garden wall'd around
Chosen and made peculiar ground;
A little spot enclosed by grace
Out of the world's wide wilderness."

(Song of Solomon 4:12–15; 5:1)
Hymn No. 13

Chapter 2

Influence of Home and School: 1685–1690 (aged 11–16).

The trials of his father made, as may be imagined, a deep impression upon the mind of the son. The adversities of his early years were doubtless remembered by him in after life.

We have a letter, written in May, 1685 (when the younger Watts was nearly eleven), by Mr. Isaac Watts Snr. to his children when he was obliged to retire to London from the storm that assailed the non-conforming churches. It is most instructive as to the kind of influence he had upon Watts. We shall quote at length because of its especial value to our story.

"My dear children,

Though it hath pleased the only wise God to suffer the malice of ungodly men, the enemies of Jesus Christ (and my enemies for his sake), to break out so far against me, as to remove me from you in my personal habitation, thereby at once bereaving me of that comfort, which I might have hoped for in the enjoyment of my family in peace, and you of that education, which my love as a father and duty as a parent required me to give; yet such are the longings of my soul for your good and prosperity, especially in spiritual concernments, that I remember you always with myself in my daily prayers addressed to the throne of grace. Though I cannot speak to you, yet I pray for you; and do hope that my God will hear me, and in due time bring me to live again amongst you, if he shall see such a mercy fit to be bestowed on me or you. However, we must endeavour by patient waiting to submit to his will without murmuring; and not to think amiss of his chastening us, knowing that all his works are the products of his infinite wisdom, his designs are the advancement of his own glory; and his ends towards his people their sanctification and salvation, which certainly shall be accomplished at last, however his great providences may seem contrary to it, as to our apprehensions.

My dear children, since in this my absence from you, it is the desire of one of you, that is, my eldest son, (Isaac Watts, junior), to have a line of counsel from his father,

1st. I charge you frequently to read the holy scriptures; and that not as a task or burden laid on you, but get your hearts to delight in them: there are the only pleasant histories which are certainly true, and greatly profitable; there are abundance of precious promises made to sinners, such as you are by nature; there are sweet invitations and counsels of God and Christ, to come in and lay hold of them; there are the choice heavenly sayings and sermons of the Son of God, the blessed prophets and apostles. Above all books and writings account the Bible the best, read it most, and lay up the truths of it in your hearts: therein is revealed the whole will of God, for the rule of man's faith and obedience, which he must believe and do to be holy here and happy hereafter. Let all the knowledge and learning you attain by other books, both at school and at home, be improved as servants to help you the better to understand God's word. The sum of all the counsel I can give you, necessary for the regulating of your behaviour towards God and man, in every station, place and condition of your lives, is contained in that blessed word of God.

2dly. Consider seriously and often of the sinful and miserable estate you are in by nature, and that you are liable to eternal wrath thereupon; also think of the way of fallen man's recovery by grace, according to the foundation-principles of the true Christian religion, which you have learned in your catechism; and beg of God by prayer to give you understanding in them, and faith to believe in Jesus Christ, and a heart willing to yield obedience to his gospel commands in all things.

Though you cannot tell how to pray as you should do, nor in any order, yet be not afraid nor ashamed to try. Go aside, my dear children, and think in your minds, what it is that you want to make you holy and happy. Tell God that you want pardon of sin, a soft, tender, and sanctified heart, a portion of the spirit, etc.; and then beg God to help you to pray for those things, and to teach you to pray, and to pardon the iniquities of your prayers. My children, though it may want a form of words, yet if the heart be in it, this is prayer, and such prayer too as God will hear and accept; for he despises not the day of small things, nor little ones, but loves to see them come and tell him what they would have. Tell him you would pray better, but you cannot, till he pleases to help you. My children, if you do but use this way, you shall find that in time you will come to have praying gifts and praying graces, too; 'for to them that ask it shall be given.' (Matt. 7:7).

3rdly. Learn to know God according to the discoveries he hath made of himself in and by his word, in all his glorious attributes and infinite perfections; especially learn to know him in and through the Lord Jesus Christ, and to be acquainted with this blessed Redeemer of God's elect.

4th. Remember that God is your Creator, from whom you received life and being; and as such you are bound to worship him; much more when you consider that he is your Benefactor, from the fountain of whose goodness all your mercies come. Now, upon both these accounts, the best of your time and abilities are required in his service; and the earlier you begin to devote yourselves to his service, the abler you will be to perform it acceptably, the greater will be your honour here, and your glory hereafter; though you must not expect to merit aught at his hands, by way of merit for what you can do, yet certain it is, that Jesus Christ will reward everyone according to his works; and we are bidden to look to the recompense of reward, in that sense after Moses' example; and it is no small commendation and honour to be an old disciple of Christ.

5th. Know this, that as you must worship God, so it must be in his own ways, with true worship and in a right manner; that is, according to the rules of the gospel, and not according to the inventions or traditions of men. Consider that idolatry and superstition are both abominable to God.

Lastly, I charge you to be dutiful and obedient to all your superiors: to your grandfather and both grandmothers, and all other relations and friends that are over you, but in an especial manner to your mother, to whose care and government God hath wholly committed you in my absence; who, as I am sure, dearly loves you, so she will command and direct you to her utmost ability in all ways, for your good of soul and body. Consider, she is left alone to bear all the burden of bringing you up; and is, as it were, a widow; her time is filled up with many cares, and, therefore, do not grieve her by any rebellious or disobedient ways, but be willing to learn of her and be ruled by her, that she may have some comfort in seeing your obedient carriage; and it will rejoice me to hear it. Avoid bad company of wicked children; abhor swearing, lying, and playing on the sabbath-day, and all other wicked courses; so shall you grow in favour with God and man. Love one another. You that are eldest, help to teach the younger; and you that are younger, do not scorn the teachings of the elder. These things I charge and command you with the authority and love of a father. Now commending you to God, and what I have written to his blessing upon your hearts, through Jesus Christ, with my dear love to your mother, my duty to your grandfather and grandmothers, and love to all other friends, being indifferent in health, I rest your very loving father.

Isaac Watts."

Isaac, junior, followed his father closely in giving expression more fully to such thoughts when he was older. The following, penned by Isaac Watts, senior, gives an indication both of the poetic gift and convictions he handed down to his son.

> "Why do our churchmen with such zeal contend
> For what the scriptures nowhere recommend?
> Those ceremonies, which they doat upon,
> Were unto Christians heretofore unknown.
> In ancient times God's worship did accord,
> Not with traditions, but the written word;
> Himself has told us how he'll be ador'd.

Such words may appear provocative to some in these tolerant days, but they were a very mild form of retaliation in the late 17th century! In common with the dissenters as a whole he did not believe in attempting to subvert the political powers by physical means. There were no "Non-conformist plots" to blow up Parliament! The most they did was to use their pens in self-defence, and in the defence of what they believed.

Influence of School

While Watts senior was suffering, his son, as his diary tells us, was studying hard under Mr. Pinhorne. His master soon discovered his desire to learn, and, carefully stimulating and directing his genius, was frequently heard to foretell the future eminence of the boy. In a Latin 'Pindaric ode,' which Watts inscribed in his twentieth year to his tutor, he acknowledges his debt to him for his instructions, and looks back with pleasure to his early studies. Mr. Pinhorne had been vicar of Eling in the New Forest, Hants. He died in the year 1714, and a monument erected in the church of Eling, where he was buried, bears an inscription to his memory. At the time of his death, the hopes he had cherished of his pupil's future success had been fulfilled.

> "Pinhorne, permit the muse t'aspire
> To thee, and vent th'impatient fire
> That in her bosom glows;
> Fain would she tune an equal lay,
> And to her honour'd tutor pay
> The debt of thanks she owes.
> "Through Plato's walks, a flow'ry road,
> And Latium's fields with pleasure strow'd,
> She owns thy guiding hand:
> Thou too didst her young steps convey
> Through many a rough and craggy way
> In Palestina's land."

The ode continues with his reflections on the classics. He valued the study of the ancients, but added these thoughts:

"Tis all romance beneath a thought
How Hercules with lions fought
And crush'd the dragon's spires:
Alike their Thunderer I despise,
The fabled ruler of the skies,
And his pretended fires.
Thy name, Almighty Sire, and thine,
Jesus, where his full glories shine,
Shall consecrate my lays;
In numbers, by no vulgar bounds controll'd
In numbers, most divinely strong and bold,
I'll sound through all the world th'immeasurable praise.'

In his "Improvement of the Mind," he advocates the use of selections from the pages of Horace, Ovid, Juvenal and Marital. The idea which he puts forward in his ode on purifying Horace, and purging his "tainted page," he attempted to follow up himself.

Mr. Watts was for more than two years an exile from his family; and probably returned to Southampton in the year 1687, when James sought to bring the dissenters over to his views by being more lenient towards them.

Freedom of Worship

Early in 1688 King James issued a 'Declaration of Indulgence.' This enabled the members of Robinson's church, to the number of seventy, to meet once more openly for worship; and a little later, Robert Thorner, a Southampton philanthropist,[7] acquired by lease the house beyond the Bargate, and converted it into a meeting-house. On August 24th the church chose as its principal officers two elders, one of whom was Thorner, and four deacons, one of whom was Isaac Watts senior.

While he was distinguished in his youth for intellectual acquirements, he also made spiritual progress. He was taught by means of catechism from an early age in the fundamental doctrines of Christianity, and frequently read the scriptures himself. Furthermore, the whole atmosphere of his father's house and the examples of piety all played their part in influencing him. There were many prayers offered for his early conversion to God, and at the age of fifteen he obtained peace and joy through believing.

"Fell under considerable convictions of sin, 1688.
And was taught to trust in Christ I hope, 1689."[8]

These brief entries tell us much. It appears to have been a deep work in his heart. The entry following in his personal memoranda in the same year, 1689, tells us that he "had a great and dangerous sickness." We are not given any idea of what it was, but it must have made him wonder about his future. Who would have imagined the tremendous intellectual exertions he was to make through almost 60 more years!

At what time Isaac, junior, felt a call to the ministry we do not know, but an offer was made him by Dr. John Speed, the physician of Southampton, with reference to his preparation for the Christian ministry. Having observed his talents and piety, this benevolent man, together with several others, generously offered to pay for his education in an English university. Firmly attached, however, to the principles which his father professed, and for which he had suffered, this proposal he respectfully declined, saying he was "determined to take his lot among the dissenters." During the time he remained under Mr. Pinhorne's tuition, which was over ten years, he made himself master of the Latin, Greek, Hebrew and French languages; while his leisure hours at home were employed, under the parental eye, in the pursuit of biblical knowledge. A deep respect for the scriptures formed a prominent feature with him; he had been taught in all his studies to take their unerring pages with him; and 'with this pilot he safely adventured in the frail bark of reason.' Gifted with a lively fancy and a vigorous imagination, it was an advantage that his mind was thus early employed upon spiritual subjects; they helped to restrain his wilder notions, and to guard against the presumption of intellectual vanity.

Further Education

Determined to take his lot among the dissenters, and consequently to forfeit the advantages of a university education, it was then decided that Watts should go to London in order to study at the Nonconformist Academy at Stoke Newington Green, which was under the charge of the Rev. Thomas Rowe. He had been thoroughly happy at Southampton; though never strong, he had rarely been out of health, and he was devoted to his home; therefore it is not surprising that he felt some sadness when for the first time "rolling wheels" bore him away from his native town, and deprived him of "the pleasures of a parent's face." Watts moved to London to prepare for the ministry. This event is thus noticed by him in his memoranda: "1690. Left the grammar-school, and came to London to Mr. Rowe's, to study phil." etc. He was now in his sixteenth year; "such he was," Dr. Johnson observes, "as every Christian church would rejoice to have adopted."

He left his father's house, but never lost the impressions received in his home at Southampton. They had taken root in "good ground," so to speak. His father lived on for many years, and Isaac frequently returned to Southampton for his health's sake. The contact was carefully maintained. Let us, therefore, return to Watts, senior, as we conclude this second chapter. The prudence and integrity of Isaac Watts, senior, won him the respect of his townsmen, and many people were used to asking his advice. The following gives a striking example of such cases. A person in Southampton who was a stone-mason, and who had purchased an old building for its materials, went with a troubled face to the elder Watts and said, "I have had a dream, and I thought the keystone of an arch fell and killed me." Watts answered him, "I am not for paying any great regard to dreams, nor yet for utterly slighting them. If there is such a stone in the building as you saw in your dream..." "There really is," interrupted the man. "Then," continued Watts, "be very careful when taking down the building to keep far enough from that stone." The mason expressed his determination to act upon the advice, but in a moment of forgetfulness he went under the arch, and the stone fell and killed him.

His gift for poetry and his genuine faith in Christ are well-expressed in verse written at the age of 85:

"Worn with the toils of fourscore years and five,
A weary pilgrim, Lord, to thee I come:
To beg supporting grace, Till I arrive
At heaven, thy promis'd rest, my wish'd for home.
Oh! had I but some generous seraph's wing,
There's nothing should prevail to keep me here;
But with the morning lark I'd mount and sing,
Till I had left earth's gloomy atmosphere."

He served the Above Bar Congregational Church as Deacon for nearly 50 years and there is good evidence that he was the first Church Secretary. Watts, senior, died in February, 1736, but two days before, his son wrote the following letter:

"Newington, Feb. 8, 1736.

"Honoured and dear Sir,

'Tis now ten days since I heard from you, and learned by my nephews that you had been recovered from a very threatening illness. When you are in danger of life, I believe my sister is afraid to let me know the worst, for fear of affecting me too much. But as I feel old age daily advancing on myself, I am endeavouring to be ready for my removal hence; and though it gives a shock to nature, when what has been long dear to one is taken away, yet reason and religion should teach us to expect it in these scenes of mortality and a dying world. Blessed be God for our immortal hopes through the blood of Jesus, who has taken away the sting of death! What could such dying creatures do without the comforts of the gospel? I hope you feel those satisfactions of soul on the borders of life, which nothing can give but this gospel, which you taught us all in our younger years. May these divine consolations support your spirits, under all your growing infirmities; and may our blessed Saviour form your soul to such a holy heavenly frame, that you may wait with patience amidst the languors of life, for a joyful passage into the land of immortality! May no cares nor pains ruffle nor afflict your spirit! May you maintain a constant serenity at heart, and sacred calmness of mind, as one who has long past midnight, and is in view of the dawning day! The night is far spent, the day is at hand! Let the garments of light be found upon us, and let us lift up our heads, for our redemption draws nigh. Amen."

It would be fitting to close this second chapter with verses from one of Watts's well-known hymns that will reflect the spirit with which he and his family faced these early years. In spite of all the distress and inconvenience they cheerfully went on, and Watts himself prepared for his great work.

"Awake, our souls! Away, our fears!
Let every trembling thought be gone!
Awake, and run the heavenly race
And put a cheerful courage on."

Hymn No. 16.

Fenchurch Street, London, in the time of Watts

Chapter 3

At College in London, and back Home: 1690-1696 (aged 16-22).

And so, the young Isaac left the Provinces and his native town for the Metropolis, where he spent four years. The journey today can be completed in 70 minutes by train, but the 75 miles or more would have taken far longer in Watts's day. The roads were primitive, since the majority were maintained by a system that went back to Tudor times. Local parishes were obliged to keep them up by the use of compulsory labour. The result was predictable: scores of roads were little more than mud tracks and in winter became torrents or bogs in which carts were stranded, and coaches broke their axles. John Wesley recorded that many a time only the sound of church bells saved him from being lost on his journey. Because of the state of the roads a great mass of trade, even grain and coal, was carried by pack-horses. The fastest coach was three days travelling from Manchester to London. The journey to London must have been wearisome for Isaac. The first regular stagecoach between Southampton and London did not begin until 1720.

What did he find when he arrived? The city was far smaller, both in size and population, than now, but it dominated the rest of the country to an even greater degree than today. The population was 675,000, and growing only slowly, out of a national population of 5¼ million for England and Wales. It was not much above three miles from East to West. It was about one mile in depth along the north bank of the Thames. To the south, only Southwark, across London Bridge, had any significance. London surpassed her nearest English rivals, Bristol and Norwich, at least 15 times in number of inhabitants. Her merchants and markets dominated the commerce of the country, "sucking the vitals of trade to herself." It was the boast of the men of Bristol that they alone kept their trade independent of London. The port of London had captured nearly all the East India trade of the country, most of the European, Mediterranean, African and much of the American.

Life in the capital was unhealthy. When Watts became pastor at Mark Lane he was frequently obliged to move out of the city, and eventually left altogether because of the effect it had on his health. The great mass of the people lived under the most filthy conditions of overcrowding without sanitation, police or doctors, far beyond the help of charity, education and religion. The death rate was appalling, and was rising because of the cheap gin that was becoming available. In the 1720's it overtook the birthrate for over a decade. The London mob was formidable, being the largest and least manageable in the Island. Hogarth's famous pictures give us a realistic estimate of conditions. Even the honest workmen in the ranks of unskilled labour were totally without education. Isaac Watts' concern for the furtherance of the cause of education was but part of a growing desire to meet the need. A leading personality among the bargemen confessed to Calamy, a leading Presbyterian minister, that he and his companions "had never so much as heard who or what Christ was," though they could easily be encouraged to burn down the meeting-houses of the dissenters or "Popish Chapels," according to the political requirements of the hour! Life was still very cruel. An advertisement of this time says: "A mad bull to be dressed up with fireworks and turned loose. A dog to be dressed up with fireworks all over and turned loose with the bull. Also a bear to be turned loose and a cat to be tied to the bull's tail."

While the conditions of the working class were miserable, life for the wealthy was attractive. London was the centre of English literary and intellectual life, of fashion, law and government. Many came from the provinces for the "London season." They hired houses in a fashionable part of the town and brought their families with them. Educated people prided themselves on their broad-minded optimism. It was "the age of enlightenment." Society was not being convulsed by political upheaval. Society had become "polite," and Christianity "reasonable." The clergy were careful to avoid the "enthusiasm" of a former age, and preaching was highly developed as an art. Butler's "Analogy of Religion" made the theory of probability and induction from nature the best evidence of Christian belief. Large numbers of the clergy were absent from their parishes, while many livings were deliberately left vacant by their patrons. However, the political element in Anglicanism was at its height. It was wedded to the Tory party, as Dissent was to the Whigs.

There were those, however, who were not satisfied with the state of affairs. The "Society for the Reformation of Manners" was a typical organisation of this period. Its ranks were open to Churchmen and Dissenters alike, and its activities were most effective in curbing the outward expression of moral decadence. Scores of thousands of tracts were issued against drunkenness, swearing, public indecency and Sunday trading. Others went beneath the surface, and philanthropy was beginning to engage in a programme of hospital building. While municipal life was at its lowest ebb, Hospital foundation was beginning as the outcome of individual initiative, co-ordinated voluntary effort and subscription.

Independent Chapels

The chapels of the Dissenters were well filled at this period, and flourishing in general. The denomination Watts belonged to was growing the fastest, and remained the least affected by false teaching. The Independents were soon to overtake the Presbyterians as the most influential of the dissenting bodies. There were about 250 Independent churches in England and Wales, with congregations averaging about 300. The figure of 75,000 may not sound large today, but out of $5\frac{1}{4}$ million brings us to the figure of $1\frac{1}{2}\%$ of the population. The equivalent today would be $\frac{3}{4}$ million.

The Academy of Newington Green was one of a number of colleges originally set up by ministers excluded from the Church of England. Since only Anglicans were allowed to enter Oxford or Cambridge, this course was inevitable. The academic standard was very high, and attempts were made by the Establishment to close them. However, they served an excellent purpose, and flourished until the last century, when the Universities were opened up to students of all denominations.

Watts had come to London, but he had very little contact with its inhabitants. Newington was on the outskirts, a village surrounded by cornfields. It is not surprising, therefore, that we do not read of bouts of ill-health in Watts' personal memoranda during his college life. The great houses of the village were occupied by London merchants and members of the learned aristocracy of Puritanism. These were the people he met in his student days. Afterwards, in his capacity as tutor, and pastor of a city church, he moved most of the time among the élite of Puritan Non-conformity. They were the stately and learned society, pervaded with memories of the great personalities of the Civil War and the Protectorate.

Daniel Defoe had been a student at Newington Green, and Watts had other well-known personalities as fellow-students. With his desire to learn, the opportunity to improve his mind was a great moment in his life. Above all, he was preparing for the ministry of the church of Jesus Christ. Sir Isaac Newton was 48 when Watts came to London. He had discovered the Law of Gravitation 28 years earlier, and was pursuing his notable career. John Locke, the philosopher, was 68, and had influenced the thinking of the head of the academy to some degree, and was to influence Watts too.

The Academy was closely associated with the Independent church that met at Girdler's Hall, Bassishaw, now Basinghall Street, and on Sunday mornings the students worshipped there. The Rev. Thomas Rowe was minister of the church as well as head of the Academy. Watts became as closely attached to Rowe as he had been to Pinhorne, and in later years, recalling the happy years spent at Newington Green, he wrote:

> "I love thy gentle influence, Rowe,
> Thy gentle influence, like the sun,
> Only dissolves the frozen snow,
> Then bids our thoughts like rivers flow,
> And choose the channels where they run."

Fellow Students

Among Watts's fellow-students were Daniel Neal, later famous for his history of the Puritans; Samuel Say (son of the ejected minister of St. Michael's, Southampton), Watts' shy and diffident schoolmate; Joseph Hort, who conformed and rose to be Archbishop of Tuam; the thoughtful John Hughes, remembered by his papers in the Tatler, the Spectator and the Guardian; and towards the end of his period there, John Shute Barrington, afterwards Viscount Barrington – a lifelong friend. Watts, Say, Hort and Hughes were drawn together by kindred tastes, and particularly by a common love for the masterpieces of Greek, Latin and English literature.

Each member of the group of four wrote in verse, and several of the poems inspired by the friendship have been preserved – written by Watts and addressed to Hort. The quadruple friendship lasted lifelong. There were many literary duels between members of the little coterie!

Hungering after knowledge and yearning to be abreast of the age in letters, Watts applied himself to his studies, for he agreed with his friend Hughes that men lack industry rather than time or abilities. He worked at fever point. Among his unwise habits was that of studying far into the night, and his continued vigils wrought havoc on a frail constitution. The dwindling candle was followed by dwindling health. Insomnia succeeded and for years, in order to obtain sleep, he was obliged to use sleeping pills. He realised too late his mistake. "Midnight studies," he said in a sermon, "are prejudicial to nature, and painful experience calls me to repent of the faults of my younger years."

In order to improve himself as a preacher he attended the most gifted ministers of the day; and he spoke with enthusiasm of three in particular: eagle-eyed, awe-inspiring John Howe, who had been Oliver Cromwell's chaplain; Thomas Gouge of the meeting-house, Thames Street, and Joseph Stennett, of Pinner's Hall, orator and hymn-writer. He praised John Flavel, that "most excellent, practical and evangelical writer." He always loved the finest company, whether in actual life or in books; and spoke from the heart when he wrote:

"Let others choose the sons of mirth,
To give a relish to their wine;
I love the men of heavenly birth,
Whose thoughts and language are divine."

We can see the way in which Watts prepared for the ministry from a manuscript volume presented after his death to Dr. Gibbons, by his brother Enoch. It contains a collection of dissertations which are evidently his college exercises. These are in his own handwriting, and consist of twenty-two Latin essays, upon physical, metaphysical, ethical and theological subjects. The theses, Dr. Johnson remarks, "show a degree of knowledge both philosophical and theological, such as very few attain by a much longer course of study."

One of the methods which Watts adopted to help his studies, was to summarise the writers upon the various sciences he read, in order to impress their contents upon his memory. "I assure my younger friends, from my own experience, that these methods of reading will cost some pains in the first years of your study, and especially in the first authors you peruse in any science, or on any particular subject. But the profit will richly compensate the pains; and, in the following years of life, after you have read a few valuable books on any special subject in this manner, it will be very easy to read others of the same kind, because you will not find very much new matter in them which you have not already examined."

There was another plan practised by Watts in after-life, which it is highly probable he commenced in the years of his studies – interleaving the books he read, and copying on the blank pages extracts from other writers on the same topics. In the manuscript volume which contains the Latin theses there are two English dissertations, which he read at the meetings of his fellow-students.

One of them was prepared, according to a note prefixed to it, for "our meeting" on Saturday, July, 1693, and is founded upon the question, "Whether the Doctrine of Justification by Faith Alone Tends to Licentiousness?." It is important as a statement of the theological views, and shows his firm grasp of and adherence to the central doctrines of the Reformation. What he wrote was not new, but merely the expression of what was held in common both by church and dissent, as can be seen by looking both at the 39 Articles and the Non-conformist Confessions. The great points of difference lay in the matter of Church Government, not in matters of faith. He develops the basic Gospel message that through the entrance of sin into the world man has fallen, and his nature has become corrupt, so that he is unable to "turn and prepare himself by his own natural strength and good works to faith and calling upon God" (Article 10 of the 39 Articles). Consequently, "We have no power to do good works, pleasant and acceptable to God, apart from the grace of God." This condition makes the salvation accomplished by Jesus Christ upon the cross necessary in order that we may be accepted by God. His good works alone can satisfy God's justice. The shedding of His blood alone can cancel out our sin. The benefits of His righteous living and death for sinners only become ours through personal faith. This is all developed by Isaac Watts. In saying these things he was giving expression to what was commonly accepted by both Dissent and Church.

He later summarised this doctrine beautifully in the familiar hymn:

"Not all the blood of beasts,
On Jewish altars slain,
Could give the guilty conscience peace,
Or wash away its stain.
But Christ, the heavenly Lamb,
Takes all our sins away;
A sacrifice of nobler name,
And richer blood than they.
My faith would lay her hand
On that dear head of Thine,
While like a penitent I stand,
And there confess my sin.
My soul looks back to see
The burden Thou didst bear,
When hanging on the accursed tree,
And knows its guilt was there.
Believing, we rejoice
To see the curse remove;
We bless the Lamb with cheerful voice,
And sing His wondrous love."

putting the very doctrine into the worship of the people of God. He expresses similar thoughts in his hymn on the Atonement (No. 20).

In the year 1692, young Watts visited his family and friends in his native town.

"Paid a six weeks visit to Southa. 1692."

The first letter which he wrote home after his return to college contained a poetical apology for its delay. It was his custom to break forth into verse whenever the occasion gave him the opportunity.

PREFACE OF A LETTER, WRITTEN AUGUST, 1692.

"E'er since the morning of that day
Which bid my dearest friends adieu,
And rolling wheels bore me away
Far from my native town and you;
E'er since I lost through distant place
The pleasures of a parent's face,
This is the first whose language sues
For your release from waxen bands;
Laden with humble love, it bows
To kiss a welcome from your hands:
Accept the duty which it brings,
And pardon its delaying wings."

A letter to his brother, Richard Watts, wishing him safety and peace in God illustrates how real and spontaneous was this personal faith in Jesus Christ that he had previously delivered in theological terms. He had not just absorbed doctrinal teaching that had little personal meaning.

"Dear Brother,

"I had a second receipt of a letter from you perhaps in the very moment in which mine came to hand; and the very day in which you was writing to me, was the same which awakened my pen to the discharge of its epistolary duty to you. We bear not the fraternal name in vain, for the same spirit possesses, inspires, and produces the most harmonious movements in us. May our mutual affection every day increase and flourish. God grant his love may purify and kindle our souls! Thus shall we in a divine manner burn with reciprocal flames of friendship. Let us contemplate our Saviour, that celestial and adorable example of love." Then he breaks into verse in his characteristic way. We shall quote only part of the poem:

"The Son of God, descending from the skies,
Assum'd an human form, that in our flesh
He might endure the agonizing pains
Due to our crimes: our surety he became,
Transferring to himself each baleful curse
Of Heaven's vindictive, death-denouncing law,
And made our guilt and punishment his own."

"I received a letter yesterday, acquainting me that our mother was somewhat better, though the fever has not quite left her. I intended to have written more particularly, but the swelling and growing verse have prevented me, and contracted the limits of my letter. Farewell, dear brother, and may you make strenuous advances in the study of religion and medicine! Given from my study in London on the sixteenth of the Kalends of February, 1693."

Reason and Religion

We remarked that Watts used to correct and illustrate the authors he read. He did this to "A Treatise of Humane Reason," printed 1675. In the title he inserted the author's name, M. Clifford, Esq., and in the blank leaf at the beginning he put his own name. His comments are very valuable as he was himself a man of great learning and saw the danger of relying on his own intellectual powers rather than upon God's Revelation. We should remember also that Watts lived in "the age of enlightenment," where "Reason" was enthroned. He considers the proposition – "Reason is to be accounted that rule and guide we look for" – and remarks:

"In this matter reason is the eye, true religion is the object: all other helps, divine and human, are as the light, as spectacles, etc. Now it is impossible to see with any thing but our own eyes, i.e. our reason. Yet a clear light is also necessary, without which our eye cannot see the object, nor our reason find out the true religion."

"Therefore, reason has a great deal to do in religion, viz. to find out the rule, to compare the parts of this rule with one another, to explain the one by the other, to give the grammatical and logical sense of the expressions, and to exclude self-contradictory interpretations, as well as interpretations contrary to reason. But it is not to set itself up as a judge of those truths expressed therein which are asserted by a superior and infallible dictator, God himself; but reason requires and commands even the subjection of all its own powers to a truth thus divinely attested; for it is as possible and as proper, that God should propose doctrines to our understanding which it cannot comprehend, as duties to our practice which we cannot see the reason of; for he is equally superior to our understanding and will, and he puts the obedience of both to a trial."

Watts needed to think this whole matter through without either losing his faith or abandoning his reason. Because he succeeded, his influence on his contemporaries was very great. He was well suited to combat the forces of scepticism and infidelity. In the Academy the cultivation of literature was blended with theological and scientific research, and the composition of Latin verses seems to have been a frequent recreation. But Watts did not allow the study of profane antiquity to usurp the place of the oracles of God; his poem "Exercitatio Cordis Coelum verses," ("the Excitation of the Heart towards Heaven"), written about this period, sufficiently proves that the spirit of devotion was not neglected for the genius of poetry. He seems to have watched with a holy jealousy over himself, lest in the gratification of a literary taste, he should lose sight of the all-important truths of the gospel, and fail to connect the improvement of the heart with the cultivation of the mind.

Joins the London Church

Isaac Watts was never a member of the church at Southampton, and it was not until some time after his departure from home that he joined a church. This took place in the year 1693, his third year at the academy.

"I was admitted to Mr. T. Rowe's church . . . Dec. 1693."

The period of his academic life ended at the beginning of the year 1694, and as he believed for some years that God had called him to the ministry, it might have been expected that he would at once have entered a pastorate. He was fully prepared intellectually, and in terms of experience he was fully qualified for the work, but it was over two years before he entered upon his calling.

Returns to Southampton

He was now twenty years of age, sixteen of which had been occupied with classical pursuits and the studies connected with theological education. In natural philosophy, the higher branches of mathematics, and the learning of ecclesiastical antiquity he was well-versed; among the dissenting communities he was already known as a youth of great promise; and his settlement with a church would doubtless have been speedily effected, had he been willing to agree to it. He observes in his memoranda, upon leaving Mr. Rowe's, "Dwelt at my father's house 2 years and ½." It is difficult to give any other reasons for this long period of silence, than the timidity and diffidence which strongly marked his character, his comparative youth, and a deep impression of the importance of the task before him. Dr. Gibbons remarks, "He returned to his father's house at Southampton, where he spent two years in reading, meditation, and prayer: in reading, to possess himself of ampler knowledge; in meditation, by which he might take a full survey of useful and sacred subjects, and make what he had acquired by reading his own; and prayer, to engage the divine influences to prepare him for that work to which he was determined to devote his life, and upon the importance of which he had a deep sense upon his spirit."

He loved to consider the works of God, and at this period of his life he was a diligent student of natural phenomena. The universe presented to his eye a varied manifestation of God; in the great and in the minute he loved to trace the wonder-working hand of the Omnipotent; and "day unto day" and "night unto night" spoke in his ear of supreme intelligence and power. His hymns are full of thoughts concerning the great works of God. His sister, Mrs Brackstone, has told how during his stay at his father's house, he endeavoured to inspire in his younger brothers and sisters a taste for similar pursuits, and to lead them to "look through nature" to the great Original. It is probable that some of the pieces afterwards published under the title of "Miscellanies" were the fruits of the leisure enjoyed at Southampton. It was probably at this time that he wrote the lines on his favourite theme, which begin:

> "My God, I love and I adore:
> But souls that love would know Thee more.
> Wilt thou for ever hide, and stand
> Behind the labours of Thy hand?"

Hymn Singing in Southampton

During this period in Southampton he would have entered fully into the life of the local Independent congregation at Above Bar. He would have been regularly in his pew with his family. The psalms sung at the Southampton meeting-house seem to have been taken from the version of Sternhold and Hopkins. This left much to be desired, as was the case with most of the earlier renderings. One day, after returning from meeting, Watts complained strongly against the roughness and general poverty of the psalmody, which he declared to be entirely wanting in the dignity and beauty that should characterise every part of a Christian service. "Try then," said his father, "whether you can yourself produce something better." Animated by the suggestion, Watts at once applied himself to the task, and after a while, composed what became the first hymn in Book 1 of his Hymns and Spiritual Songs:

> "Behold the glories of the Lamb,
> Amidst His Father's throne:
> Prepare new honours for His name,
> And songs before unknown." No. 18.

And so he began the work for which he is best remembered, the writing of hymns. It was fitting that it should begin in a practical setting. He was composing to meet a real need. It was appropriate that it should begin in Southampton, the place where he had received so much, in his father's home. He was ready for this great work. His mind was prepared, the situation called for it, and he had leisure to write. So the great torrent began. It is clear, we shall see, that it all started in Southampton, because it was as a result of his brother Enoch's famous letter that he undertook to revise the whole of Christian worship. Enoch had had a taste in the local congregation of what his brother could do. Watts was a great thinker and it has been suggested that during his stay in Southampton he used his leisure hours and the quiet of his father's house to study the whole question of worship and hymn-singing. He would have made himself familiar with the versions of the Psalms then available, and probably considered the whole principle of hymn-singing that he later developed and defended. We do not know exactly how many hymns were written then, but we do know that it was while looking across the Southampton Water from Western shore towards the New Forest that he was inspired to write later the familiar words:

> "There is a land of pure delight
> Where saints immortal reign.
> Infinite day excludes the night,
> And pleasures banish pain.
>
> Sweet fields beyond the swelling flood
> Stand dress'd in living green;
> So to the Jews old Canaan stood
> While Jordan rolled between." No. 10.

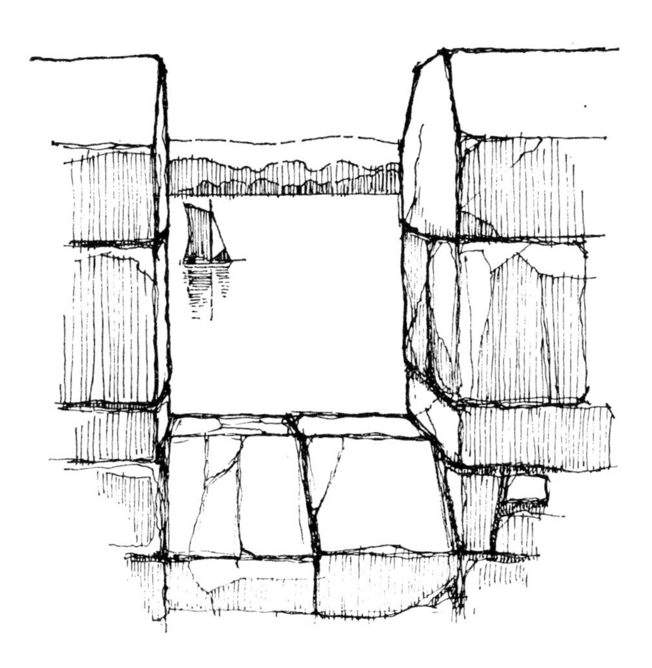

Chapter 4

Tutor and Pastor: 1696–1706 (aged 22–32).

The next entry in Watts's Memoranda tells us that on October 15, 1696 he "came to Sir John Hartopp's to be a tutor to his son at Newington." This move is hardly surprising. His abilities were well-known to the dissenting aristocracy. He moved to a sphere where he could not only be of service to Sir John but pursue his studies with another real situation before his eyes. His thinking could develop still further as he sought to instruct the family. His great mind did not restrict itself to teaching the children, but had a wider public in view. It was, however, an excellent starting point, as later in the case of the Abney household. The scholar could be fulfilled, while at the same time be intensely practical. The practice itself would complement and enlarge his studies. It kept him from useless and remote intellectual exercise.

Sir John had several houses, the principal one being Fleetwood House, Church Street, Stoke Newington. He and his wife Elizabeth had a son, John, and six daughters. Sir John, who had an estate at Freeby, near Melton Mowbray, in Leicestershire, had been parliamentary representative and High Sheriff of that county.

Previous to the accession of William III, he had, like all other prominent Dissenters suffered severely for his faith to the tune of several thousand pounds. Watts pays glowing tributes to him "When I name Sir John Hartopp," he says, "all that knew him will agree that I name a gentleman, a scholar and a Christian. He had a taste for universal learning. But the Book of God was his chief study and his divinest delight; his Bible lay before him night and day. He was desirous of seeing what the Spirit of God said to men in the original languages; for this end he commenced some acquaintance with Hebrew when he was more than fifty years old. His doors were ever open, and his carriage was always friendly and courteous to the ministers of the Gospel. He was a present refuge for the oppressed, and the special providence of God secured him and his friends from the fury of the oppressor. He often entertained his family in the evening worship on the Lord's day with excellent discourse, some of which he copied from the lips of some of the greatest preachers of the last age." When speaking Sir John was occasionally overcome with emotion. His eyes would moisten and his "voice would be interrupted, and there would be a sacred pause and silence." With all the members of Sir John's circle Watts was on agreeable terms. To Watts, teaching was no trial. He regarded it, indeed, as a joy – as one of the noblest of occupations. "How lovely is it," he says, "to see a teacher waiting upon those that are slow of understanding, and taking due time and pains to make the learner conceive what he means without upbraiding him with his weakness." It was all right for Watts to speak in this way with a teacher-pupil ratio of 7 to 1. Had he the problem of facing a class of 30 to 40 in a difficult area his frail constitution may well have collapsed! To some schoolmasters he once said, "Youth, my dear friends, is the time to acquire knowledge; and as you have the important charge laid upon you of instructing some of the rising generation, let me beg, as you wish well to your precious and immortal soul, that you will leave nothing undone to make your pupils love the beauties of religion. Teach them that religion has nothing in it of a gloomy nature; for how can that be gloomy which leads to everlasting pleasures?" Watts frequently dwelt on the theme of "cheerful piety;" the second verse of his hymn "Come we that love the Lord" echoes this thought.

The sorrows of the mind
Be banished from the place;
Religion never was designed
To make our pleasures less.

V. 2 No. 18.

This was so true of the thinking of the man. While he did not believe Christianity should ever be robbed of its spiritual and holy character in order to make it attractive, he was ever at great pains to make the vehicle by which it was carried simple and straightforward. This delight in education stayed with him all through his life.

Mark Lane Independent Church

Sir John Hartopp and his wife were members of a church which met in Mark Lane, one of the most famous streets in London.

Their pastor was the Rev. Isaac Chauncey, a learned man. The church did not prosper under his ministry, however. Mark Lane, with which Watts was destined to be closely connected for twelve years (1696–1708) was in those days a street of handsome houses, some of which might even be described as palaces. They were the homes of the opulent merchants who had gained their wealth chiefly through trading in corn and wine in the market. Samuel Pepys, the diarist, was a familiar figure in the neighbourhood at the time it was frequented by Watts.

While with the Hartopps, Watts still had his mind on improving the worship in church and meeting-house. The friendship between Say and Watts proved to be one of the influences which caused him some years later to apply himself seriously to the work of "imitating" the Psalms. Say and Watts had often criticised severely the older metrical versions; and Say not only wrote paraphrases to some of the Psalms, but submitted them to both Watts and Hughes. This was at the end of 1697. Watts's letter of acknowledgement is lost, but Hughes replying on 6th November, 1697, said, "I give you my hearty thanks for your ingenious paraphrase, in which you have so generously rescued the noble Psalmist out of the butcherly hands of Sternhold and Hopkins." Further than this, Say did not go, but he had conceived the idea of paraphrasing the whole of the Psalms. The entire scheme began to progress in Watts's mind.

On 17th July, 1698, his birthday, Watts delivered his first sermon, and in the following month he preached several times at Southampton. Sometimes he accompanied the Hartopps to their Leicestershire seat, Freeby, and conducted services in the ancient stone meeting-house in the village. Later, two stained-glass windows were inserted, one on each side of "Dr. Watts's pulpit." In that to the left Watts is shown in a preaching gown and looking upon a cross – "the wondrous cross on which the Prince of Glory died;" in that to the right is "Mistress Mary Hartopp."

Above the former is the inscription:-

Dr. ISAAC WATTS IN THIS BUILDING PREACHED THE CROSS OF CHRIST; above the latter,

HE WAS TUTOR AT THAT TIME TO MISTRESS MARY HARTOPP OF FREEBY.

Owing to Dr. Chauncey's dullness in the pulpit and tactlessness out of it, the congregation at Mark Lane had for some years been declining. In the autumn of 1698, Watts was invited by the congregation, through Sir John Hartopp apparently, to become assistant pastor, in place of the Rev. Edward Terry, who had retired through age. He began his ministry in Feb. 1699. In general Watts preached in the morning, and Dr. Chauncey in the afternoon; as a result of the change, the lifeless cause began to revive. As a pastor, Watts was almost all that could be wished. He was an orator, and his sermons were invariably fresh, thoughtful, and stimulating; indeed, the only complaint the congregation made against him was that they saw too little of him in their homes. We notice this in one of his lyrics,

"The noisy world complains of me
That I should shun their sight, and flee
Visits, and crowds, and company."

Unhappily, he was frequently in bad health, and sometimes confined to his room for days by illness.

By this time he had become a close friend of Sir Thomas Abney and his wife, who then lived at Highgate Hill. Sir Thomas Abney, who early in life had cast in his lot with the Nonconformists, was a power in the city of London. His first wife, Sarah, daughter of the Rev. Joseph Caryl, died in 1698, and in 1700 Sir Thomas married Mary, eldest daughter of Mr. John Gunston.

To Thomas Gunston, Lady Abney's brother, Watts became deeply attached, and he was a frequent visitor at Gunston's home, in Church Street, Stoke Newington, an ancient mansion standing in beautiful grounds. Nearly all the people with whom Watts came into contact were men of affluence, the merchant princes of London. Their houses, or rather their palaces, were furnished with elegance. They shone at home and abroad in silks and silver. They had "chariots" and horses, "and rich equipage." They were without pride and were not ostentatious. They had great wealth, but they used it wisely. Their "splendid frugality," to use John Hughes's phrase, was proverbial. This was however a comparative frugality, we might add. They were powers in Mark Lane and Lombard Street. Among these men the fashionable vices of the day were unknown.

Watts and Gunston loved to walk and unbend to each other under a row of "reverend elms" that were the glory of Mr. Gunston's grounds; in the "wilderness," as, according to the custom of the day, the shrubbery was called; or in the trim gardens that crept up to the house with their lordly cedars and their quaint topiary work. Most gentlemen's gardens in those days possessed a mound "a very agreeable piece of elevated ground whence could be surveyed the neighbouring fields and meadows covered with cattle" and there was a very picturesque mound in Mr. Gunston's grounds, an attractive spot that overlooked a sheet of ornamental water and a heronry. Watts was entranced by it, and in later years, when the estate took the name of Abney Park, this mound, "Watts's Mount," as it was afterwards known, became his favourite retreat. Watts indeed, again and again, both in prose and verse, draws his illustrations from lawn and garden—birds and blossoms, and the rich dark shadows of heavily-leaved trees. This was the era of "Capability Brown," the famous landscape gardener. He got his name from the habit of saying he saw "capability of improvement in an estate." The grounds at Newington were typical in every way of contemporary landscaping.

In 1700 Mr. Gunston took down the old house and erected near its site, and amid its cedars and yews, a trim red-brick, geometrical mansion, crowned with a turret. The walls of one of the front rooms upstairs – the Painted Room, as it was called – were embellished with paintings, in gilt mouldings, illustrating Ovid's Metamorphoses, one of them, that over the fireplace, being a representation of Actaeon turned into a stag, with water in the foreground. When the artist was away at dinner, Watts, who had inherited from his grandfather and father some ability with the brush, happening to be in a mischievous mood, painted on the water a swan, and was amused afterwards by the artist's expression of surprise. A back staircase ascended not only to the upper rooms, but also to the turret, which was a favourite haunt of the two friends. There on a bench they

"alone would sit,
Free and secure of all intruding feet,"

and converse on literature, religion, art and science. Watts's environment was far removed from the squalor of the masses in London, but he was well qualified to influence the higher ranks of society, and this he did.

Mayor's Chaplain

On becoming Lord Mayor of London Sir Thomas Abney had appointed Watts his chaplain. In those days no one could take high office unless he was willing to receive the sacrament of the Lord's Supper at a Church of England table, and Sir Thomas, who had no objection to "Occasional Conformity," complied with the custom. Sir Thomas's action in respect to the sacrament gave the Jacobite party an opportunity for furious invective, and when striking at Sir Thomas they did not omit a passing slash at Watts. Their pamphleteers were of the opinion that "Sir Tom" would have been much better employed singing "Psalms at Highgate Hill" and "splitting texts of Scripture with his diminutive figure of a chaplain." Sir Thomas's action also gave offence to many of the Dissenters, including Daniel Defoe, who called it "a-playing at bo-peep with God Almighty."

Sickness returned to Watts and for five months he had to lay aside his work. Afterwards he visited his family at Southampton, to "try his native air" for the recovery of his health. Having referred to his settlement with Dr. Chauncey, he observed:-

"And a little while after my fever and weakness began,
Paid another visit to Southampton of five weeks.
.... July 1, 1699.
"Another .... June, 1700.

The illness of Watts returned in the summer of 1701, and from June to November he was wholly incapable of preaching.

"Went to ye Bath by ye advice of Physicians, June 9, 1701.
"From ye Bath to Southampton............ July, 1701

"Thence to Tunbridge.................... Sept. 3, 1701.

"Returned to Newington Nov. 3, and to
preaching at Mark Lane, ... Nov. 1701.

Dr. Chauncey had at last the wisdom to see that owing to his own inability to cope with affairs only one satisfactory course lay before him, that of retirement, and on 15th April, 1701, "to ye great surprize of ye Church" he sent in his resignation. And it was high time, for the membership had dwindled from 171 to 74. The eyes of the worshippers were at once directed towards Watts, but "he objected warmly" and frequently "his indispositions of body" which incapacitated him from much service," eventually after some improvement in health he agreed. He wrote two letters to the church by way of reply. The first dealt with the matter of the functioning of the church. The second was a personal acceptance of the call. This was on 8th March, 1702.

"On March ye 29th" continues the Church Book, "Our Pastor admrd ye Lord's Supper amongst us, having preached ye foregoing Thursday a preparatory Sermon from 1 Cor. 10, 17; wherein he shewed how much our communion with each other as well as with Christ was set forth and sealed in this great Ordinance, designing to unite all ye hearts and affections of ye church to each other, yt ye day of Communion might be as a new Covenant with ye Lord and with each other also. We finished ye celebration of ye Lord's Supper by singing a Gospel Hymn suitable to ye Ordinance, taken from Rev. 1st 5, 6, 7, with one heart and one voyce, to ye glory of our Redeemer and our great consolation and joy." This was Hymn 61 in Watts's 1st Book, and that time unpublished – the first verse of which runs:

"Now to the Lord, that makes us know
The Wonders of His dying love,
Be humble honours paid below
And strains of nobler praise above."

Watts seems to have resided with Sir John Hartopp till 1702, when he moved to the house of Mr. Thomas Hollis near the chapel in Mark Lane. In this house he had a "technophyon" or "secret chamber" at his command to which he could "retire from the world and converse with God and his own heart;" holding to the belief that a room of this kind is "a most considerable advantage for improvement in godliness." Here he daily examined himself, probing the depths of his soul. Here he prayed and wept. Here he drew down his strength. "Abandon the secret chamber," he says, "and the spiritual life will decay."

Watts's congregation appreciated his labours; and its numbers continued to increase. Whenever ill-health prevented him from taking a service he would send a pastoral letter, and these writings are as attractive as the character which they faithfully mirror.

In 1703 Watts again suffered a long and distressing illness, and the church with a view to lightening his duties, appointed him an assistant in the person of the Rev. Samuel Price; a modest, gentle, kindhearted, but occasionally indiscreet minister, who won the confidence of Watts, and worked with him harmoniously. Finding that he could not be a great man, Price aimed at being a good man, and he succeeded.

In August, 1703, Watts being again out-of-health paid another visit to Tunbridge Wells, and after his return, finding it impossible to continue his literary labours without assistance, he hired a lad to write for him.

Watts had many distinguished friends, among whom was the eldest daughter of General Ireton, and grand-daughter of Oliver Cromwell. Occasionally Watts came into touch with Richard Cromwell, who resided at Cheshunt, and was a member of John Howe's church in Silver Street. Watts recalled him as a white-haired old man with a polished and impressive way of speaking, and observed, "I never heard him glance at his former station but once, and that in a very distant manner." In January the oldest member of the Mark Lane Church died, Mrs. John Owen, widow of the Rev. Dr. John Owen; and the event carried men's minds back to the period of the Laudian persecution and to the days of the Protector.

Watts was constantly in touch with his relations in Southampton, and one of his letters to his sisters Sarah and Mary – has been preserved. It shows us his deep concern for his nearest and dearest and his capacity for sympathizing.

"Dear Sisters,

"Read the love of my heart in the first line of my letter and believe it. I am much concerned to hear of my mother's continued weakness. We take our share in these painful disorders of nature, which afflict her whom we honour and love. I know also that your hurries of business must be more than doubled thereby; but we are daily leaving care and sin behind us. The past temptations shall vex us no more: the months which are gone return not, and the sorrows which we hourly feel lessen the decreed number. Every pulse beats a moment of pain away, and thus by degrees we arrive nearer to the sweet period of life and bliss.

"Bear up, my dear ones, through the ruffling storms.
Of a vain vexing world, tread down the cares,
Those ragged thorns which lie across the road,
Nor spend a tear upon them."

Sisters,

Accept the sudden rapture kindly, the muse is not awake every day. If she has a moment's release from the lethargy, see, 'tis devoted to serve and please you—etc.

"June 15, 1704.

Pinners' Hall, Old Broad Street, London

When the chapel in Mark Lane became dilapidated, Watts's congregation removed in June, 1704 to Pinners' Hall, Old Broad Street. On 2nd April, 1705, John Howe died. Watts used to say that there was one passage in Howe's writings which he often read with ecstatic pleasure, and felt that he could always be reading – that passage in which are portrayed the joys in store for us "when death shall have discumbered and set us free from all sorts of distempers, and brought us into the state of perfect and perfected spirits," and when "all shall be full of divine life, light, love and joy, and all freely communicate as they have received freely." His own writings in prose and poetry frequently dealt with this theme – it is not surprising therefore that he was so affected.

Watts had at various times written quite a number of poems, and he at last decided to issue them with the title of "Horae Lyricae" (poems chiefly of the lyrical kind). The volume appeared in 1705. In his preface, he deplores the fact that the art of verse which was first consecrated to the service of God should so often have been prostituted to the vilest purposes, to give gay colours to temptation, and gild over the foulest images of iniquity; and he tells us that his aim in publishing the book was to remove this reproach and to restore poetry to its highest and noblest use. This, indeed, was his aim all through life. He loved, for example, to take heathen poems and to give them a Christian tone. He insisted on the importance of using sparkling images and magnificent expressions. The Prophets, he says, should "be read incessantly, for their writings are an abundant source of all the riches and ornaments of speech," and this he considers far better counsel than that of Horace, who bade those who would excel in poetry, study night and day the Greek models.

Among Watts's memoranda occurs the entry, "Went to Southampton 18th May, 1706, returned again with but small recruit of health July 5th." "There is a land of pure delight," was written during this visit. He kept in touch with his family, and wrote to his brother Enoch a letter that throws some light on the views then held by non-conformists. See Appendix I.

There now entered into Watts's life the beautiful and accomplished Miss Elizabeth Singer. Her father who, like the Elder Watts, had been imprisoned for Non-conformity, lived near Frome, but he and his family were frequently in London; and they were connected with several persons of rank. Miss Singer paraphrased, at the request of Bishop Ken, the 38th Chapter of Job. She was of medium height and build and just Watts's age, had fine auburn hair, and dark blue eyes that sparkled with animation. Her complexion was very fair, and a "lovely blush" glowed in her cheeks. She moved with grace, and her voice was "harmoniously sweet." She was fond of "sticking flowers in her hair." She told him in verse that, enchanted by his verse, her thoughts no longer occupy themselves with her old admirers and desired to meet him. Her wish was at last granted. But before her stood not even a moderately presentable Englishman, but a minute, sallow-faced anatomy with hook nose, prominent cheekbones, heavy countenance, pale complexion and small grey eyes, which, however, when he gazed upon her, filled with sparkles. Her heart sank within her; and Watts's heart must have sunk too, for no man was better skilled than he in reading the thoughts of others. But if, on account of his plainness, she at first recoiled from him, the variety and charm of his conversation swiftly compensated for her disappointment, and she congratulated herself on having made the acquaintance of a man whose friendship would be as precious to her as his love was distasteful. The sight of Miss Singer stirred in Watts tender feelings which he had supposed would never disturb him; and he could not prevent amatory lines from appearing in his poems. "Perhaps," he wrote in the preface of the 2nd edition of Horae Lyricae, "there are some morose readers that stand ready to condemn every line that is written upon the theme of love; but have we not the cares and the felicities of that sort of social life represented to us in the sacred writings? Is it utterly unworthy of a serious character to write on this argument, because it has been unhappily polluted by some scurrilous pens?" When at last Watts summoned up sufficient courage and proposed to her, she declined him, though in her sweetest manner, adding, not very happily, if with the best of intentions, "Mr. Watts, I only wish I could say that I admire the casket as much as I admire the jewel."

Watts, however, accepted the situation with sweetness and amiability, and as he could not, in the phrase of the day be her servant he was content to be her friend. He was bound to be affected by the disappointment and tradition will have it that Watts's experience was responsible for the suspicion of pique in Hymn 48, Book 2, entitled, "Love to the creatures dangerous."

"How vain are all things here below!
How false, and yet how fair!
Each pleasure hath its poison too
And every sweet a snare."

It is unlikely, however, that Watts was a very ardent lover. In any case the wounds healed quickly and beautifully, and his subsequent friendship with Miss Singer proved to be one of the most pleasing episodes in his career. There is another anecdote that relates to his appearance. He was once in a coffee-room with some friends and overheard a gentleman remark contemptuously at his appearance,

"What! is that the great Dr. Watts?"

With admirable presence of mind and good humour he turned and repeated some of his own verse:

"Were I so tall to reach the pole,
Or grasp the ocean with a span,
I must be measured by my soul.
The mind's the standard of the man."

Elizabeth Singer

Chapter 5

Preacher and Evangelist 1706–1709 (aged 32–35).

Isaac Watts had become pastor of a famous church. Joseph Caryl (author of the lengthy commentary on the book of Job) had been the first minister in 1662. He was followed by Dr. John Owen, whose neighbouring congregation united with the one he adopted as pastor. Nineteen years after he died Watts became minister. The congregation had declined and Watts's ministry fulfilled expectations that the work would flourish again. The congregation was obliged to move from Mark Lane because of the state of the building to Pinners Hall. Watts lived close at hand and was able to give his full attention to the work, in spite of repeated bouts of ill-health.

While this particular congregation was growing, the scene in many of the churches was depressing. Perhaps there has been no period since the Reformation, when the ministry of religion in the Establishment exercised so little beneficial influence upon the people. The church, in the language of Archbishop Leighton, was "a fair carcase without a spirit"; the clergy, according to Burnet, were "the most remissin their labours, and the least severe in their lives of any in Europe." Dr. Southey indeed tells us, that "from the Restoration to the accession of the house of Hanover the English church could boast of its brightest ornaments and ablest defenders, men who have never been surpassed in erudition, in eloquence, or in strength and subtlety of mind." This was true: but the very powers with which they were gifted were used to reduce Christianity to a philosophical system, and convert religion into a moral scheme. With all their Ciceronian eloquence and Attic purity they were apostles of natural religion, rather than preachers of the revealed word – more familiar with Plato than Paul, with the ethics of Seneca than with the glories of the cross.

Among the Dissenters the Presbyterians were in serious decline. There was among them a tendency to expand their subjects to their widest extent; not merely to illustrate the general sentiment of the text, but to eke out a meaning from its minutest parts, and if possible extract a lesson from the most obstinate word and barren particle. Their preaching was doctrinal. The Independents on the other hand were expository in their preaching and the most successful of the dissenters. The General Baptists were in decline as were the Quakers, but the Particular (Calvinistic) Baptists were generally in a flourishing condition. Their preaching was commonly of an experiential character.

Unity

Viewing this scene Watts printed in 1707 an "Essay against Uncharitableness." One edition was published, though a reprint was often called for: it was soon after incorporated in a larger work, entitled, "Orthodoxy and Charity united." Watts was grieved that Christians were so often separated by points of doctrine that could only be considered secondary. But he would not tolerate compromise on "essentials" of the faith.

By "orthodoxy" the author understood all those doctrines which were generally received and professed by Protestants at the Reformation: and he advocated the extension of a fraternal love towards all those who agree here, however widely in other respects they may differ. He did not believe in sacrificing the Word of God at any point for the sake of Unity, but believed that Christians could get closer together than they were in his day.

He maintained his link with his native town. It benefited his health.

"Went to Southton. July; returned July. Went to Tunbridge, Aug; returned Sept. 3.

"All this year my health has been increasing.

"Overturned in a coach without hurt, Oct. 5, 1707.

We saw earlier the part played by "the societies for the reformation of manners." On Oct. 6, 1707, Watts preached a sermon for them and had it printed. The reformation societies were certainly doing much good; many of the asylums of vice, by their means, were broken up; and a striking improvement in the public morals was soon visible. "England," says a contemporary writer in the year 1706, "bad as she is, is yet a reforming nation. Let any man look back to the days of King Charles II, when rampant vice overran the court, when all sort of lewdness spread over the face of authority. Let him view the example of the late royal pair; let him look into the examples now reigning, and tell me. Is it nothing to dethrone the devil and depose his agents? To disarm the factors of hell, and banish rampant vice?"

French Prophets

At this time the religious world was disturbed by some French emigrants who claimed to possess the miraculous gifts of the Holy Spirit, and to be the founders of a new dispensation of religion. The power of working miracles, and the gift of prophecy, they advanced as the credentials of their divine mission. "This fancy," says Calamy, had been at work in France, in 1703, and many fell with it. These people in France were called Camisars and strange and incredible stories were spread abroad concerning them. They were very fond of prophetical impulses, and abounded among the new converts in the Cevennes in the South of France. It was reported they were there guilty of great irregularities. They were vehemently opposed and run down, and at length suppressed. Some of them coming into England in 1706, with great vigour and earnestness endeavoured to spread their views here, where they were but too well entertained. They said that a new prophetic dispensation was to be proclaimed in every nation under heaven, beginning in England, and to be manifest over the whole earth within the short term of three years.

Watts took notice of the event. "This year ye French prophetts made a great noise in our nation, and drew in Mr. Lacy, Sir R. Bulkley, and 200 or more had ye agitations, 40 had ye inspiration. Proved a delusion of Satan at Birmingham, Feb. 3 or 4, 1707-8."

Sir Richard Bulkley, here mentioned, was a gentleman of considerable wealth and learning, which he employed spreading the views of the Gallic prophets.

Being deformed in person, he fully expected under the new dispensation to be made straight in a miraculous way; an event which to his great grief did not occur. He wrote in vindication of his party, and was answered by Calamy and Hoadley. Mr. Lacy was a member of Dr. Calamy's own congregation at Westminster; his alliance with the enthusiasts led him to immorality which he tried to justify from Scripture. The whole imposture was discovered soon, for the prophets declared that one of their followers would rise from the dead on a specified day to confirm the truth of their pretensions, and it did not happen! While these strange events were taking place, and churches generally were in decline, Watts was among those who pursued his work faithfully and successfully. There were many such congregations, concerning most of whom we know very little. However, Watts was at the centre of things and his ability was well known.

Watts as a Preacher

As a preacher he ranked high among his contemporaries; his printed discourses establish his claim to eminence in this respect. He carefully adapted himself to the least intelligent, yet never in such a way as to offend the educated and refined. There was always a rich vein of good sense, and profitable instruction in his sermons, adorned with occasional gleams of vivid imagination. Some rose against him with the accusation of legalism yet he proclaimed with unabated earnestness the duties as well as the blessings of the gospel, and advanced the threatenings of the Lord with the free invitation of His grace. He ever kept in mind the great object of his office, "to feed the church of God" not to amuse the idle, to please the curious, or to gratify the learned.

In 1708 the meeting-place was moved to Bury Street. It was small at the beginning of his ministry but increased considerably under his care, and many additions were made to the church of those who were "his glory and joy."

> "Sweet is the work, my God, my King,
> To praise Thy name, give thanks and sing:
> To show Thy love by morning light
> And talk of all Thy truth at night"

No. 3.

In the pulpit he had none of the advantages of an imposing personality, commanding voice, or elegant gesticulation. It might truly be said, that his bodily presence was weak. He made use of little or no action. His voice was rather too fine and slender, but regular, audible, and musical. But in spite of his low stature his appearance when preaching is said to have been remarkably dignified: his manner was unaffectedly grave and solemn. His enunciation was distinct, accurate, and easy, always pleasing by its cadence, but impressive when the subject required it. "I once," says Dr. Johnson, "mentioned the reputation which Mr. Foster had gained by his proper delivery to my friend Dr. Hawkesworth, who told me that in the art of pronuncation he was far inferior to Dr. Watts." His general mode of sermonising was to prepare an outline of his subject, which he took with him into the pulpit, and trusted to his extemporary powers to fill up the sketch. In early life he prepared with greater care, and almost entirely wrote out his sermons. At the close of his sentences, when any thing more than ordinarily important was treated of, he frequently paused a little, to give his hearers opportunity for reflection. With a boundless fertility of imagination, and complete command of language, he was never hurried, seldom vehement. He maintained a perpetual control over himself and his subject.

Simplicity

One of the chief qualities of his mind was clarity, but it cannot be said that it was a great virtue of the preachers of Watts's youth and early manhood. Watts was anxious to have the congregation not only sing with understanding but hear with understanding too. He tried to reform the preaching of his day, especially the structure of sermons. He began his ministry in an age of what he calls happily "branching sermons." Even pulpit giants like Owen and Howe could exhaust their mighty energies and their hearers by the minute sub-divisions of their sermons. Watts tells us that he had sat under this method of preaching until he had thought of Ezekiel's vision in the valley full of bones: "behold they were very many and very dry." In another place, he says "Preachers talk reason and religion to their auditories in vain, if they do not make the argument so short as to come within their grasps, and give a frequent rest to their thoughts." He pruned his own sermons as ruthlessly as he did his hymns, that they might be direct, simple in structure, and understood by the ordinary worshipper.

"Bless'd be the Lord, who comes to men
With messages of grace;
Who comes in God his Father's name
To save our sinful race."

Verse 4. Hymn No. 5.

Dr. Gibbons wrote "In prayer it might perhaps be truly said, that he excelled himself. It was throughout an address to Deity, not in florid expressions, but in easy and unadorned language, and rather short and weighty periods. There was an extent in his addresses to Deity, which comprehended every proper subject, and at the same time such a brevity that at the conclusion of his prayer a hearer might find himself at a loss to conceive what more or less could have been said."

In the early part of his ministry, Watts gave a series of lectures upon prayer to a private society of young men, who met together in the vestry of his meeting-house for devotional fellowship. Too often prayer lacked plainness and simplicity, and was marred by a rough and familiar speech with the use of dark and mystical phraseology. Prayer should be accompanied by the adoration of the divine perfections, a deep gratitude for the blessings of this life and for the expectation of a better; prayer should be conducted under an awful sense of the divine presence, and ought to be an acknowledgement of our dependence upon One who "knoweth our infirmities before we ask, and our ignorance in asking" – it should not assume the character of demand. These lectures were published in 1716 under the title "A guide to prayer."

He was not content, however, to be simply expert in the pulpit. He would visit and apply personally what he had said in his messages. He used every opportunity which conversation offered of speaking of the things of God. When visiting his people in the discharge of pastoral duty, he usually took with him a number of religious tracts, to present to the younger members of their families.

The Rev. Kingsbury of Southampton told the following to Dr. Gibbons, as he received it from the mouth of Watts's son-in-law "Mr. Richard Ellcock was a servant in old Mr. Watts's family. Upon Dr. Watts's returning to London after visiting his father at Southampton, Richard Ellcock was sent with him a day's journey. Dr. Watts entered into conversation with him, which made a deep and lasting impression on his heart, and was the means of his sound and saving conversion. After he came to London he wrote to his father, recommending his servant for that he believed he would make an eminent Christian and so he lived and died, leaving an honourable character for piety and uprightness behind him. This is attested by many." Watts was not out to make a reputation for himself but simply to point men to his master the Lord Jesus Christ. And was always ready to do this personally. However, he was fond of studious retirement, and so devoted to his books, that in the early part of his career he seldom went out. Sickness afterwards frequently made it impossible. But in his seasons of health and vigour, when thrown into company, and drawn out in conversation, his society was always interesting and profitable. His conversation was such as in all respects became the man of wisdom and the man of God. As he was never anxious to draw attention to himself, so neither was he inclined to run down others. He had his opponents, and those who sought to represent him in the most disadvantageous light; but he did not retaliate.

In his common conversation he never appeared to be at any loss for thought or expression. "Indeed, no person," says Dr. Gibbons, "with whom I was ever acquainted spoke with more ease, readiness, and elegance than he did; and, as his discourse flowed like a clear full stream from an inexhaustible fountain, so it was very instructive and entertaining. I have collected some proofs of this kind, the much greater part of which are taken from the register of my own memory."

He recalled such words of wisdom, "I could wish young ministers in the country might be allowed by their people to read a part of Mr. Henry's exposition of the bible, or repeat a sermon from some good author, one part of the Lord's days, as it is certainly too much for them to compose two sermons a week so early in life"—"Never mind spoiling a well-turned period if you may but have the hope of reaching a conscience. Polished and harmonious language is oftentimes like oil flowing smoothly over marble, which leaves no traces behind it."—"I had rather be the author of Mr. Baxter's 'Call to the Unconverted', than the author of Milton's 'Paradise Lost'."

Here we have the proof of his calling to the ministry. His greatest concern was to preach the gospel. There must have been many saved through his ministry. Samuel Medley the hymn-writer tells of an occasion when he went to hear Watts preach, simply to please a friend. At first he was not interested and found the message irksome but as the preacher dealt with the opening of blind eyes the words entered his heart and he was given grace to repent and believe.

"How beauteous are their feet
  Who stand on Sion's hill!
Who bring salvation on their tongues,
  And words of peace reveal!"

Hymn No. 17

Chapter 6

Poet and Hymn-writer: 1707–1718 (aged 33–44).

Isaac Watts was born in the same year that John Milton died and there are many similarities between them. This is so regarding their upbringing and training, but above all in their concept of the work of a poet. Watts must have studied Milton intensely, and admired him greatly. They both believed that the poet's work was a divine calling.

His poems (Horae Lyricae) had been published in 1705 and because they were so well received on both sides of the Atlantic a second edition appeared four years later. Many of his poems must have been composed while he was at Southampton since some bear the date 1694 and others as early as 1691. He saw his poetic gift as the handiwork of devotion. He rarely touched any topic but to pass it into service, his torch was kindled with the fire from the altar, if he visited Parnassus it was only on the way to Calvary. His aim was not simply to please but to convert the seeker. We saw earlier that he said that he would rather have written Baxter's "Call to the Unconverted" than Milton's "Paradise Lost." Unlike Milton he was a Minister and his calling to preach the Gospel was ever in his mind. This did not cast a gloom over his writings as some would wrongly imagine. He always carried with him and his writings a cheerful spirit. His "cheerful piety" was an example to all who read his works. The poems were his finest works and Dr. Johnson considered that they entitled him to an honourable place amongst his "English Poets."

Reference has already been made to Dr. Johnson and it is striking that such a literary figure should have had such a high view of Watts. England had already seen 150 years of the finest literary production of her history when Dr. Johnson achieved his fame. It was the "age of enlightenment" and culture was valued by the upper classes of society. Many celebrated literary men used to gather around Dr. Johnson in one of the 3,000 coffee houses that existed in his day. They were popular with citizens, merchants, writers and lawyers as places of social resort. Here a newspaper could be borrowed for a penny and local news was passed on by word of mouth. They crowded round Dr. Johnson to hear his words of wisdom on a vast range of topics. His comments were so valued that Joshua Reynolds founded a club that met once a week "in order to give Dr. Johnson unlimited opportunities of talking." There must have been many occasions when he expressed his high opinion of the various works of Isaac Watts. This would have made a great impact on the literary world.

While Watts was still busy with his poems he was also preparing his hymns. His collection of poems included a sample of 200 hymns ready for publication. He was testing out the willingness of the Churches to adopt hymns in their worship. It is difficult for us to realize the novelty of such a practice. He had to be cautious and he was.

His poems appeared in a number of editions and each time he fashioned, discarded and refashioned his material until he had produced the modern English hymns for popular use. The term "genius" has been defined as "an infinite capacity for taking pains." Watts would certainly qualify for such a term on this basis.

The first edition of "Hymns and Spiritual Songs" appeared in 1707 and his preface referred to the need of Reformation in modes of preaching and prayer, and adds "of all our religious solemnities Psalmodies is most unhappily managed." He set a good example in preaching, not only by delivering excellent messages, but by having them published. He also gave directions regarding prayer and published his "guide to prayer." His greatest work of reformation, however, related to worship.

We need to go back again to Southampton to see how it began, for though he saw well enough the need to improve the worship at the local meeting-house, it was his brother Enoch who wrote to him from Southampton pressing him to set about the great task of changing the whole form of worship. It is an historic letter and is preserved. Enoch surely claims some share in Watts's great work for though Isaac was slow to respond, Enoch had sowed the seed. The letter was written in 1700 and it took seven years to bear fruit. Isaac was naturally diffident, but also wanted to be sure he was doing the right thing. Above all he wanted to be thorough.

Southampton March 1700

"Dear Brother,

In your last you discovered an inclination to oblige the world by showing it your hymns in print; and I heartily wish as well for the satisfaction of the public as myself, that you were something more than inclinable thereunto. I have frequently importuned you to it before now, and your invention has often furnished you with some modest reply to the contrary, as if what I urged was only the effect of a rash and inconsiderate fondness to a brother. I am very confident, however, that whoever has the happiness of reading your hymns will have a very favourable opinion of their author, so that, at the same time you contribute to the universal advantage, you will procure the esteem of men the most judicious and sensible.

Furthermore, consider how very mean the performers in this kind of poetry appear already. There is great need of a piece vigorous and lively as yours, to quicken and revive the dying devotion of the age, to which nothing can afford such assistance as poetry, contrived on purpose to elevate us even above ourselves. Yours is the old truth, stripped of its ragged ornaments, and appears, if we may say so, younger by ages, in a new and fashionable dress.

As for those modern gentlemen, who have lately exhibited their version of the Psalms all confess to me a vast difference to yours, though they are done by persons of no mean credit. Dr. Patrick most certainly has the report of a very learned man, and, they say, understands the Hebrew extremely well, which indeed capacitates him for a translator, but he is thereby never the more enabled to versify. Tate and Brady still keep near the same pace. There is in them a mighty deficiency of that life and soul, which is necessary to raise our fancies and kindle and fire our passions. I have been persuaded to a great while since, that were David to speak English, he would choose to make use of your style. If what I have said seems to have no weight with you, yet you cannot be ignorant what a load of scandal lies on the dissenters, only for their imagined aversion to poetry. You remember what Dr. Speed says:

"So far hath schism prevail'd, they hate to see
Our lines and words in couplings to agree,
It looks too like abhorr'd conformity:
A hymn, so soft, so smooth, so neatly drest,
Savours of human learning and the beast."

And, perhaps, it has been thought there were some grounds for his aspersion from the admired poems of Ben. Keach., John Bunyan, etc., all flat and dull as they are; nay, I am much out if the latter has not formerly made much more ravishing music with his hammer and brass kettle.

"Now when yours are exposed to the public view, these calumnies will immediately vanish, which methinks should be a motive not the least considerable. Lastly, if I do not speak reason, I will at present take my leave of you, and only desire you to hear what your ingenious acquaintance at London says to the point, for I doubt not you have many solicitors, there, whose judgements are much more solid than mine. I pray God Almighty have you in his good keeping, and desire you to believe me.

"My dear brother,
"Your most affectionate kinsman and friend"
"ENOCH WATTS."

Enoch's letter provides useful commentary on the mode of worship in his day. There *were* versions of the Psalms, but they were most unsuitable. Hymns too had been written, but Watts was the first to see the need for a complete reformation in worship. Benjamin Keach, the pastor of the Baptist Church at Southwark (this eventually became the church that called C. H. Spurgeon to be their pastor in the 19th Century) approached the nearest to Watts of all his forerunners. He was the first dissenter to publish a hymn-book to meet the needs of a definite congregation. He also shared Watts's view of the purpose of hymns, both as an instrument of praise and also of instruction. Keach, however, was content to meet the local needs, whereas Watts wanted to change the worship of the churches at large! His reformation meant an almost complete departure from traditional psalmody. When this was later realised many who had enthusiastically supported him forsook his standard. Watts's logic and some of the need for truly Biblical worship drove him to a complete root and branch reformation.

We need to see the change he brought about to appreciate what a great work he performed. The churches believed that Psalm singing was the basic form of sung praise. Hymns were never written to replace them, but to supplement them and then only on occasions. Watts saw the weakness of this, not simply because the translations were clumsy and the method of singing poor, but above all because it impoverished true worship. But he carried out his work gently and by stages.

He proposed the re-creation of the traditional psalmody along evangelical lines. He knew that he would be under fire and sought in his comprehensive way to deal with all the objections he expected would be raised against his new scheme. He anticipated that he would be accused of "tampering with God's Word." He ensured that it remained intact and was good for instruction. It was another matter to expect sung praise which was a response to that Word, to be the Word itself.

He pointed out that even when the Psalms of David were used in Old Testament worship, it was improbable that they were *all* used. Thus he implied a criticism of those who put the whole Psalter into verse for public worship. He forestalled the objection that there was no need to omit and amend parts of the text of the Psalm. He knew that some would say that the worshippers could interpret them in a gospel manner as they sang them, but answered that in public worship there was a need for something approaching a uniformity of interpretation.

His belief that the Psalms were to be handled in this way did not arise because of any doubt that they were all inspired by God. Neither did he believe that the meaning should be altered in any verse, but should rather be *developed* in the light of the fuller New

Testament revelation. When he said that David should use the language of a Christian he was not implying that David was in any way "unchristian," but rather "pre-Christian." He saw a perfect *harmony* between the revelation of the Old Testament and the New. He saw the inconsistency of preaching and praying in the name of Jesus Christ and at the same time excluding this title from sung praise. He believed that he was simply calling for a return to the New Testament worship where the Christians were exhorted to make melody in their hearts "in the name of the Lord Jesus Christ" (Gal. 5: 19, 20).

Watts in his study at Abney House

Watts succeeded in his great task. He not only pointed out the need for reform, but presented the churches with large numbers of suitable hymns. These not only supplied a need, but served as models and examples for later hymn-writers. Watts acted pastorally in what he was doing. He saw that Christians need to understand what they are singing and to offer to God praise that is worthy. His view of worship was thoroughly Biblical. In a preface to his "Psalms and Hymns" he tells us just what he has done and why. We shall quote it in full since Watts needs little editing as he was always brief and to the point.

Extract from Dr. Watts's Preface.

"I come therefore to explain my own design, which is, to accommodate the book of Psalms to Christian Worship and in order to this, it is necessary to divest David and Asaph of every other character but that of a Psalmist and a saint and to make them always speak the common sense and language of a Christian.

Attempting the work with this view, I have entirely omitted

several whole Psalms, and large pieces of many others; and have chosen out of all of them, such parts only as might easily and naturally be accommodated to the various occasions of the Christian life or at least might afford us some beautiful allusion to Christian affairs. These I have copied and explained in the general style of the Gospel; nor have I confined my expressions to any particular party or opinion: that in words prepared for public worship, and for the lips of multitudes, there might not be a syllable offensive to sincere Christians, whose judgments may differ in the lesser matters of religion.

Where the Psalmist uses sharp invectives against his personal enemies, I have endeavoured to turn the edge of them against our spiritual adversaries, Sin, Satan, Temptation. Where the flights of his faith and love are sublime, I have often sunk the expressions within the reach of an ordinary Christian: where the words imply some peculiar wants or distresses, joys or blessings, I have used words of greater latitude and comprehension, suited to the general circumstances of men.

Where the original runs in the form of prophecy concerning Christ and His salvation, I have given an historical turn to the sense; there is no necessity that we should always sing in the obscure and doubtful style of prediction, when the things foretold are brought into open light by a full accomplishment. Where the writers of the New Testament have cited or alluded to any part of the Psalms, I have often indulged the liberty of paraphrase, according to the words of Christ, or His apostles.

New Testament Terms

And surely this may be esteemed the Word of God still, though borrowed from several parts of the Holy Scripture.

Where the Psalmist describes religion by the fear of God, I have often joined faith and love to it. Where he speaks of the pardon of sin through the mercies of God, I have added the merits of a Saviour. Where he talks of sacrificing goats or bullocks, I rather choose to mention the sacrifice of Christ, the Lamb of God. When he attends the ark with shouting into Zion, I sing the ascension of my Saviour into Heaven, or His presence in His church on earth.

Where he promises abundance of wealth, honour, and long life, I have changed some of these typical blessings for grace, glory, and life eternal, which are brought to light by the Gospel, and promised in the New Testament. And I am fully satisfied that more honour is done to our blessed Saviour by speaking His Name, His graces, and actions, in His own language, according to the brighter discoveries He has now made, than by going back again to the Jewish forms of worship, and the language of types and figures."

As we bear in mind what he has written, we shall see for ourselves how it has all worked out when we sing the hymns he wrote that are familiar to us.

The hymns that were originally written for the independent meeting-house have been taken up by all denominations. We may not have realised that we were singing one of Watts's Psalms paraphrases when we have sung "O God our Help," or "Jesus shall reign."

We can illustrate just how Watts went about his task if we look at some of the hymns we have in Appendix V. We have selected 20. This selection is based on an analysis of 52 Anglican hymn-books that give an account of the 325 "standard hymns of the highest merit according to the verdict of the whole Anglican church." We have used this selection deliberately in order to indicate how widely Watts is still sung and to make use of well-known hymns to illustrate our points. We shall see just what Watts meant in his preface.

His paraphrase of Psalm 136 which begins:

"Give to our God united praise:
Mercy and Truth are all His ways
Wonders of grace to God belong
Repeat His mercies in your song."

No. 7.

illustrates the point he makes in his preface admirably. In Psalm 136 each verse ends "for His mercy endured forever," whereas Watts alternates the third line of each verse with "wonders of grace to God belong" and "His mercies ever shall endure," whereas Milton with his "Let us with a gladsome mind" repeats the same two lines in each verse,

"For His mercies shall endure
Ever faithful ever sure."

After paraphrasing a large number of the Psalms and rendering the deliverance of the Jews from Egypt in verse he gives us the fuller *typical* interpretation of the event in the "language of a *Christian*."

"He sent His Son with power to save
From guilt and darkness and the grave."

He finally rounds off the paraphrase that speaks of God's physical provision for His people with a *spiritual* message:

"Through this vain world He guides our feet
And leads us to His Heavenly seat."

With his Psalm 117 we have another example of the introduction of Gospel terms and thought into the language of the Old Dispensation. Its brevity give us space for a careful comparison.
Psalm 117: "O Praise the Lord, all ye nations; praise Him, all ye people. For His merciful kindness is great towards us and the truth of the Lord endureth forever. Praise ye the Lord."
Watts puts it:

1. "From all that dwell below the skies
Let the creation's praise arise:
Let the Redeemer's name be sung
Through every land by every tongue."
2. "Eternal are thy mercies Lord
Eternal truth attends Thy Word
Thy praise shall sound from shore to shore
Till suns shall rise and set no more."

Scriptural Paraphrasing

A good example of the way in which he gives a wholesale interpretation to a Psalm is his treatment of Psalm 122. Here we have David going up to Jerusalem as a worshipper and he is changed into a Christian going to church. The Psalm that begins: "I was glad when they said unto me, let us go into the house of the Lord. Our feet shall stand within Thy gates O Jerusalem," becomes

"How pleased and blessed was I
To hear the people cry,
Come let us seek our God today!"
Yes, with a cheerful zeal
We haste to Zion's hill
And there our vows and homage pay."

No. 6.

Many dissenting places of worship were named "Zion" and both Churchmen and dissenters have thought of a local church as the "house of the Lord." Watts proceeds through the Psalm so as to make it apply exactly to worshipping in a local church.

In another familiar hymn:

"Come let us join our cheerful song
With Angels round the Throne
Ten thousand thousand are their tongues
But all their joys are one."

No. 12.

we have a paraphrase of Revelation 5, v 11–13. Here there is no need to interpret the text with the fuller light of a further revelation. For Watts the New Testament could not be added to. Consequently he simply puts the passage freely into verse.

Watts kept close to Scripture and consequently there is great variety in his hymns. His talent and experience were so comprehensive that he could do justice to the many subjects that were to be handled. He surpasses the "poet of Methodism," Charles Wesley, by being the servant of the Universal Church.

He travels with the Christian through all his varied experiences, from the new birth to the glory of heaven. There is a hymn for every season and every occasion. C. H. Spurgeon would bear witness to this fact. As a young man he learnt many of Watts's hymns by heart and found a great use for them in later life.

He tells us in his autobiography, "My grandfather was very fond of Dr. Watts's hymns, and my grandmother, wishing to get me to learn them, promised me a penny for each one that I should say to her perfectly. I found it an easy and pleasant method of earning money, and learned them so fast that grandmother said she must reduce the price to a halfpenny each, and afterwards to a farthing, if she did not mean to be quite ruined by her extravagance. There is no telling how low the amount per hymn might have sunk, but grandfather said that he was getting overrun with rats, and offered me a shilling a dozen for all I could kill. I found, at the time, that the occupation of rat-catching paid me better than learning hymns, but I know which employment has been the more permanently profitable to me. No matter on what topic I am preaching, I can even now, in the middle of any sermon, quote some verse of a hymn in harmony with the subject; the hymns have remained with me, while those old rats for years have passed away, and the shillings I earned by killing them have been spent long ago."

And so Watts completed his greatest work for the Christian church. He was only 44 and was yet to write much more, but it was almost entirely prose. The hymn-writer died, as it were, in 1718. We have overlapped our history in this chapter with the next but have done so in order to pursue our theme.

If we had to choose one hymn out of all that he wrote that would express his own heart it would surely be the one that has meant more than any other to a great many people. While "O God our help" is the best known of his hymns, the following is surely the deepest and best loved. It has been described by Matthew Arnold as "the greatest hymn in the English language."

"When I survey the wondrous Cross
On which the Prince of glory died
My richest gain I count but loss
And poor contempt on all my pride."

No. 9.

Chapter 7.

Trials and Conflicts: 1709–1720 (aged 35–46).

Isaac Watts had many advantages not afforded to the dissenters in general, and was able to set quietly to work on his great task while many were suffering continued persecution. We read in his personal memoranda:

"March 1, 1710. ye Mob rose and pulled down ye pews and gallery of 6 meeting-houses, but were dispersed by ye guards at 1 or 2 in ye morning."

We need to go back a little to see the cause of the trouble. There was considerable feeling among some High Churchmen at the success of the Dissenting academies, and a cry was raised for their suppression. A clergyman, Dr. Henry Sacheverall, was prominent in promoting this move. He sought to revive old fears by harking back to Cromwell and the execution of Charles I, and represented the academies as being hotbeds of sedition. He was encouraged in this attitude by Charles Wesley's father, who had been a Dissenter himself, and had become very bitter against them. He pressed for the suppression of "such a growing mischief." It was also asserted that "they endangered the success of the two national Universities," and that far more of the gentry would have sought their education there but for these "sucking academies." There was little attempt at self-defence by the Dissenters, with one notable exception, that of Daniel Defoe. He met the attacks with a satire that was so delicate that it completely deceived those against whom it was directed. This was the age of satires such as "Gulliver's Travels."

Defoe began his "The Shortest Way with the Dissenters" with a history of Dissent in which its rebellious tendencies were exaggerated and a tyrannical character given to them. The "purest Church in the world," he said, has borne it with "inimitable patience" and a "fatal leniency." He gave reasons for dealing with them once and for all, and answered objections. "They are numerous, but so were the Huguenots, and yet the French king disposed of them; the more numerous they are the more dangerous." "This is the time to pull up this heretical weed of sedition that has long disturbed the peace of our church and poisoned the good core." Is it cruel, he asks, to do this? "Is it cruel to kill a snake or a toad?" "I do not prescribe fire and faggot, but they are to be rooted out of this nation." The book was eagerly read. Defoe himself said, "The wisest Churchmen in the nation were deceived by this book." Many approved of it. The skit was taken quite seriously. "I pray God," said a Fellow of Cambridge, "to put it into Her Majesty's heart to carry them into execution." Some Dissenters were taken aback. When it was discovered who wrote it, one of the Dissenters themselves, Defoe was vehemently denounced and punished. He was put in the stocks, but pelted with flowers by the people!

Controversy

Dr. Sacheverall was not to be outdone, and in 1709 sounded from the pulpit of St. Paul's a blast in his sermon "Perils of False Brethren both in Church and State," preached before the Lord Mayor and Aldermen of London on the anniversary of the Gunpowder Plot. He boldly attacked the Whigs and the Dissenters, and insisted on the people's obligation to absolute and unconditional obedience to the crown. He charged the Dissenters with "the most abominable impieties," and with justifying "murder, sacrilege and rebellion by texts of Scripture." Had he been left alone all would have been well, but he was made a martyr. He was impeached before the House of Lords. The trial lasted 10 days during which time the crowd became wild with enthusiasm for him. He was an able preacher and succeeded in stirring the mob against the dissenters. It was thus that the 6 meeting-houses were wrecked. Others were wrecked in the Midlands. But this was not the end of the matter. His attacks on the Whig Government had stirred up people's feelings, and when he was narrowly condemned and lightly sentenced it was regarded as almost an acquittal. His influence grew and the government fell.

The controversy over the position of the Dissenters still smouldered, and broke out again into flames. It was occasioned by the behaviour of Sir H. Edwin, a Dissenter who was the Chief Magistrate of the City of London. Dissenters were allowed to hold high office provided they "occasionally" took the sacrament in the Church of England. This practice had continued for some years without question, but when Sir Edwin unwisely carried the "regalia" of his office to Pinner's Hall meeting-house there was a storm. They were alarmed at the spectacle of the "ensigns of the august Corporation" being carried to a "nasty conventicle." A move was made not only to outlaw "occasional conformity," but the Dissenting academies too. In 1714 the Schism Bill was passed. It received the royal assent on June 25th. It would have closed every school and academy in the country that was not licensed by a Bishop and conformed to the liturgy.

Divine Intervention

Those were dark days for the Dissenters. The Bill was due to come into operation on August 1st. Thomas Bradbury, the outspoken Independent preacher who had been one of those whose meeting-house had been wrecked earlier, was on his way to worship that very morning, August 1st. As he walked along he was passed by Bishop Burnett, who stopped his carriage and invited him to his side. He asked the cause of Bradbury's seriousness and the reply was given, 'I am thinking whether I shall have the constancy and resolution of that noble army of martyrs who were burned to ashes in this place; for I most assuredly expect to see similar times of persecution, and that I shall be called to suffer in a like manner.' The Bishop who had been such a friend of William III and who was a very staunch Protestant, did what he could to quiet Bradbury's fears: and told him that the Queen was very ill and not expected to recover. He also said that he was going to the Palace, and would send a messenger to him with the earliest news of the Queen's death.

If it should happen that Bradbury was in the pulpit the messenger would be instructed to drop a handkerchief from the gallery, as a token of the event, Bradbury had not long to wait, for whilst he was preaching the handkerchief was dropped. He completely suppressed his feelings of emotion whilst preaching but during the closing prayer he returned thanks to God for the deliverance of these kingdoms from the evil counsels and designs of their enemies; and implored the divine blessing "upon His Majesty King George and the House of Hanover," Mr. Bradbury always maintained that he was the first man who proclaimed King George I.

THE SLUGGARD.

'Tis the voice of the Sluggard: I heard him complain,
'You have waked me too soon! I must slumber again!'
As the door on its hinges, so he on his bed
Turns his sides, and his shoulders, and his heavy head.

'A little more sleep, and a little more slumber!'
Thus he wastes half his days and his hours without number;
And when he gets up he sits folding his hands,
Or walks about sauntering, or trifling he stands.

I made him a visit, still hoping to find
He had took better care for improving his mind:
He told me his dreams, talk'd of eating and drinking
But he scarce reads his Bible, and never loves thinking.

AGAINST EVIL COMPANY.

WHY should I join with those in play
In whom I've no delight;
Who curse and swear, but never pray;
Who call ill names, and fight?

I hate to hear a wanton song:
Their words offend my ears:
I should not dare defile my tongue
With language such as theirs.

Away from fools I'll turn my eyes,
Nor with the scoffers go:
I would be walking with the wise,
That wiser I may grow.

From one rude boy, that's used to mock,
They learn the wicked jest:
One sickly sheep infects the flock,
And poisons all the rest.

AGAINST PRIDE IN CLOTHES.

WHY should our garments, made to hide
Our parents' shame, provoke our pride?
The art of dress did ne'er begin
Till Eve our mother learnt to sin.

The tulip and the butterfly
Appear in gayer coats than I:
Let me be dress'd fine as I will,
Flies, worms, and flowers exceed me still.

Then will I set my heart to find
Inward adornings of the mind:
Knowledge and virtue, truth and grace,
These are the robes of richest dress.

THE CENTRE EIGHT PAGES:

Pages (i), (ii) and (iii)
These are from an 1866 Presentation Edition of Watts's "Divine and Moral Songs".

This page (iv and v)
Tudor House Museum, Southampton
Civic Centre Clock Tower, Southampton

Page (vi)
God's House Tower

Page (vii)
Statue of Isaac Watts at the West/Watts Park

Page (viii)
Notes in Isaac Watts Bible ("Cope Collection", Southampton University Library)

Contemplations

Here lyes infolded in this booke divine
gods loue to man free graces magazine
Here lyes infolded in these sacred lines
free grace in Christ that onely mine of mines
Here lyes infolded in each page alone
Some spirituall food for saints to feed upon
Here flows that fountain that doth far excell
Euphrates streames or good old Jacobs well
Jordan floods may bee compared to this

Acrostick petitions

I mortall god in persons three
S weetly convey thy grace to mee
A id mee with wisdome from aboue
A nd compasse mee about with loue
C ouer my failings Blest Jehoue

W ash off my sins make cleane my hart
A nd righteousnesse to mee impart
T each mee to understand aright
T hy sacred word and with delight
S hall I peruse it day and night

Those who were behind the Bill were immediately in trouble and the Dissenters escaped. They did not bear malice against the Queen, feeling that she was being used by others. It was at this time that Isaac Watts wrote his famous hymn, "O God, our help in ages past. . .," which belongs to his Psalm imitations (being Psa. 90, Hymn No. 2). Dissenters felt the political issues keenly because though they did not believe in mixing politics and Christianity, they were aware of the Providence of God in history. They were thankful that the throne was now occupied by a Hanoverian. They could expect easier times under George I, and they were not disappointed.

Continual Sickness

Isaac Watts's meeting-house did not suffer through any of these trials, neither did he receive any personal abuse, but this period was for him a testing time in other ways. He had recurring bouts of illness. These interrupted his work on the "Imitation" of the Psalms, and in 1712 his health broke down. He makes his own comment on the experience:

"Amid all the violence of my distemper and the tiresome months of it I thank God I never lost sight of reason and religion though sometimes I had much ado to preserve the machine of animal nature in such order as regularly to exercise either the man or the Christian."

He refers in verse also to the horrors that accompanied this dreadful illness, observing:

> "Oh, 'tis all confusion!
> If I but close my eyes, strange images
> In thousand forms and thousand colours rise—
> Stars, rainbows, moons, green dragons, bears and ghosts."

But his most acute distress arose from the fact that he was unable to proceed with his rendering of the Psalms. "David's harp" was "ready strung for the Messiah's name," but he who would touch the chords was "confined to sit in silence," and to "waste the golden hours of youth." The illness lasted during the whole of 1713 and even on 4th November of that year, when he wrote a letter to the Church, he had but faint hopes of recovery. In it Watts warmly thanked his people for their kind support of him under a "tedious and expensive sickness," and advised as to the course they should take in case of his death.

During some of the intervals in his sickness, his conversation with friends showed his calm and submissive spirit: "I know not but my days of restraint and confinement by affliction may appear my brightest days, when I come to take a review of them in the light of heaven." To one of his friends he observed, "St. Paul's thorn in the flesh was the debilitated state of his nerves, occasioned by the overpowering glories of heaven; whence I conclude, that the apostle was in the body when he was caught up into paradise." This opinion, though completely conjectural, is a useful commentary on the nature of his own affliction, concerning which we are told very little. In a letter to a minister in affliction he thus expresses himself: "It is my hearty desire for you, that your faith may ride out the storms of temptation, and the anchor of your hope may hold, being fixed within the veil. There sits Jesus our forerunner, who sailed over this rough sea before us, and has given us a chart, even his word, where the shelves and rocks, the fierce currents and dangers, are well described; and he is our pilot, and will conduct us to the shores of happiness. I am persuaded, that in a future state we shall take a sweet review of those scenes of providence, which have been involved in the thickest darkness, and trace those footsteps of God when he walked with us through the deepest waters. This will be a surprising delight to survey the manifold harmony of clashing dispensations, and to have those perplexing riddles laid open to the eyes of our souls, and read the full meaning of them in set characters of wisdom and grace."

Co-pastor appointed

On the 3rd March, 1713, owing to Watts's continued illness, Mr. Price, his assistant at Bury-street, was ordained co-pastor with him, at his express recommendation and desire. In the dedication of one of the volumes of sermons to his people, he says that he could not conceal his joy, that his kind and faithful companion in the service of their souls practises his ministry with the same views and designs (as himself) and that he had been clearly blessed of God, to support and build up the church during his long confinement.

But there was more in this illness than he thought, for it proved to be in its result more blessed to him than any other event of his career. In the spring of 1714 Watts began to mend, and Sir Thomas Abney, who believed that fresh air and a change of surroundings would do more good than medicine, invited him to spend a week at his country seat, Theobalds, near Cheshunt, Hertfordshire. The stately mansion of Theobalds, which had been erected by Elizabeth's powerful minister, William Cecil, had been razed by the Parliamentarians in 1650, and apparently even the ruins had disappeared at the beginning of the 18th century. On the estate, however, several fine houses had been built, one of which had become the home of Sir Thomas Abney.(9) The grounds were once the finest in England, with their lakes, canals, bridges, fountains, labyrinths, terraces and summer-houses; and the portion that surrounded Sir Thomas' house still preserved some of its antique glory. When the week was over, the Abneys pressed Watts to stay longer, and finally they invited him to remain with them for good. He gladly consented, with the result that his health which had for so long been precarious, gradually returned, his emaciated body put on flesh, and his pale cheeks regained their natural colour. And so, by invisible hands, Watts was suddenly transported from a dull, austere retreat, and from the foul air of a crooked, narrow city street, to a fine English mansion under the open sky. In place of bricks and tiles and a few stunted, pent-up trees, he could, at will, feast his eyes on the crimsons and purples of gardens – the pomp of cedars of Lebanon. Whose were those invisible hands would be clear to a man of Watts's piety.

This invitation led to a residence of nearly forty years with this amiable family, by whom he was treated with the utmost kindness as a friend, attention as an invalid, and respect as a divine. "A coalition like this," Dr. Johnson remarks, "a state in which the notions of patronage and dependence were overpowered by the perception of reciprocal benefits, deserves a particular memorial." The Countess of Huntingdon once told Mr. Toplady that when she visited Dr. Watts on one occasion he thus accosted her: "Madam, your Ladyship is come to see me on a very remarkable day." – "Why is this day," she replied, "so remarkable?" – "This day thirty years I came hither to the house of my good friend Sir Thomas Abney, intending to spend but one single week under his friendly roof, and I have extended my visit to the length of exactly thirty years." Lady Abney, who was present, immediately said, "Sir, what you term a long thirty-years' visit, I consider as the shortest visit my family ever received."

In this pleasant spot Watts could continue his writing, and also attend to the family's spiritual needs. To the characters of Sir Thomas Abney, Lady Abney, and their "virtuous daughters," Sarah, Mary and Elizabeth, whose education he superintended, and whose interests were thenceforward his own, Watts paid various and warm-hearted tributes. Several of his works were written to give them pleasure, and he composed mottoes for the sun-dials in Sir Thomas' garden. In one of the rooms which had a window looking west was a ceiling or Spot Dial – an invention of Sir Isaac Newton – which consisted of a little mirror fixed in the floor so as to reflect the sun on to a dial marked on the ceiling; and Watts composed upon it the lines:

"Little sun upon the ceiling,
Ever moving, ever stealing
Moments, minutes, hours away;
May no shade forbid thy shining
While the heavenly sun declining
Calls us to improve the day."

In the fresh air

His favourite retreat at Theobalds was an alcove in one corner of the garden where he used to keep some of his books, including a choice copy of Virgil, the works of Cicero, of whom he was an ardent admirer, and the volumes of the Spectator. In this arbour-library he composed a number of his "Imitations" of the Psalms, and there are some pleasant reminiscences of it in his work, "The Strength and Weakness of Human Reason." His favourite walk led northward from Theobalds to an imposing house which, altered and enlarged, became Cheshunt College. Watts was an early riser and he could be seen walking out any morning when the early sun showed through the network of elms that skirted the park, and the cows were driven home to milking through the haze of their own breath. There are in his works many references to this habit, indeed, one whole poem, "The Lark," is occupied with the subject:

> "Night past and all the shadows fled,
> The rosy morn began t'appear;
> When I forsook my weary bed,
> And walked abroad to take the air."

His delight in the early morning is manifested also in his prose works. "Surely," he says in a sermon, "it can be no great hardship for any persons in health to begin their day with the rising sun, for almost half the year." In one of his Divine Songs he wrote:

> "This is the day when Christ arose
> So early from the dead;
> Why should I keep my eyelids closed,
> And waste my hours in bed?"

When with Watts indeed we are always in the keen, fresh, exhilarating air.

In 1717 Watts was again prostrated by sickness, and on 12th February, 1718, he wrote from Theobalds to the Church in Bury Street: "I acknowledge with much affection and gratitude your hearty love to me under my long affliction, and your continual requests to God for my restoration to you. . . . My dwelling so much in the country is so far from preventing my attendance on this church, that I find it the only means whereby I can hope to be restored to your service; for I have made a new and sufficient experiment of this lately. The good family where I have been entertained with so much kindness (and which God hath made instrumental of so much mercy to me) was confin'd in London by particular providences the last month for five Lord's days together; and it was only the first of these days that I could appear in public worship with you: the last fortnight I was reduced so low that I could seldom pray in the family. He that sees the secrets of all hearts knows the inward longings and desires I felt towards this assembly; but He that gave me this inclination is a witness of my incapacity. I wait His time, and seek and pray for submission and length of patience. . . . If you would know my present state of health, I think I am a little refreshed with the country air since I left the city six days ago; though I would be glad always to dwell among you where my chief business lies and my chief pleasure, if God saw fit to instruct me with any measure of useful strength. If there be any secret sin for which God yet contends with me, I long to have it discover'd that there might be no more cause of further contention betwixt my God and me.

"O may the good spirit of Prayer be with you that at length ye may prevail, and lay a foundation for much thanksgiving! Blessed be His name who hath thus far supported me; I long to serve Him, and I think I value my life for no other purpose: but He wants me not, nor my poor services; and however He deals with me, I joyn heartily with all your prayers for ye spiritual and eternal welfare of this church, to which I am engaged in all the bonds of love, gratitude and the Gospel. And while my worthy and beloved friends are assisting you at the mercy-seat may they obtain mercy for themselves and the churches under their care! May Divine success attend all their labours wheresoever they are called to spread ye savor of the name of Christ! and may our heavenly Father reward into all your bosoms that labour of love you are all engag'd in this day on the account of "Your unworthy and afflicted brother and servant,

"Are we the soldiers of the Cross
The followers of the Lamb?
And shall we fear to own His cause
Or blush to speak His name?" No. 14.

"I. Watts."

Chapter 8

Watts's Contribution to Education: 1720–1746 (aged 46–72).

During the years 1720 and 1721, the nation was preoccupied with the formation and proceeding of the South-sea Company. "Clergy and laity, Whigs and Tories, Churchmen and Dissenters, statesmen and ladies, turned stock-jobbers." Watts took notice of the national infatuation in his usual way.

"'Tis said, the citizens have sold
Faith, truth and trade for South-sea gold.
'Tis false! for those that know can swear
All is not gold that glistens there."

How right he was, for as we know the "South-sea Bubble" burst, and the consequences were disastrous. In one year there were 59 cases of suicide reported in London alone, besides 74 people drowned and 63 discovered dead from unknown causes. Watts felt obliged to write a "Defence against the Temptation of Self-murder."

The period, however, was uneventful on the whole. It was for Watts one of continual bodily suffering, yet extraordinary mental exertion. He made a considerable contribution to education and exhibited some very up-to-date ideas on the subject. Little had been written for children, so that Watts's works in this field were well-appreciated. It is probable that he wrote his "Divine and Moral Songs, for the use of Children" in 1720.

His "Divine Songs" have been very highly valued. It has been estimated that through the years seven million copies have been sold. It is still in print (obtainable from the Entertainments and Publicity Department, Civic Centre, Southampton), and Oxford University Press in 1971 published a special study edition with extended notes in their "Juvenile Library." It shows us that Watts is still with us, so to speak!

Watts was in an ideal setting for study and reflection, and he put it to good use. His works were appreciated in the New World, as well as in Britain. He lived either at the Abneys' home at Theobalds, in the neighbourhood of Cheshunt, near Epping Forest, or at Stoke Newington, in their other home. Let us see him hard at work in his study at Newington, spending long hours at his desk, in spite of his bodily suffering, driven by his strong desire to use his outstanding gift to the full, to the advantage of many. As we approach the door we see lines from Horace over the entrance, denouncing insincerity in friendship. On entering the room we notice the bookshelves crammed with books of all kinds. Where there are spaces we see prints hung, of notable people, particularly ministers of the Gospel. Over the fireplace there is a panel with more quotations in Latin from his favourite Horace. Not far away is a "painted room," moulded with gilt, and on the window shutter a drawing made by Watts's own pencil of emblems of mortality mingled with the family arms of Abney and Gunston (Gunston being Lady Abney's maiden name). We also see the heads of Aristotle, Alexander and Democritus painted by the same hand. In such surroundings he would be hard at work, but ready to put down his pen when he had to attend to the needs of the family. He led the daily devotions of the household, and greatly endeared himself to the servants. They were anxious to attend to all his needs.

He did not abuse these privileges but used every moment to produce pieces that have lasted many years, and in some cases are still with us. He worked hard on his "Divine Songs," and they have been well thought of. With remarkable freedom he adapted himself to the mental capacity of children. His rhymes presented a rare combination of the simple, the useful and the attractive. Perhaps they stand alone in the way that they accommodate the truth of the Gospel and duties of morality to the child's mind. Dr. Johnson remarked, "For children he condescended to lay aside the scholar, the philosopher and the wit, to write little poems of devotion, and systems of instruction, adapted to their wants and capacities, from the dawn of reason through its gradations of advance in the morning of life. Every man acquainted with the common principles of human action will look with veneration on the writer, who is, at one time, combating Locke, and at another, making a catechism for children in their fourth year. A voluntary descent from the dignity of science is perhaps the hardest lesson that humility can teach." C. H. Spurgeon highly praised Watts's catechism in his autobiography: "Dr. Watts's Catechism, which I learned myself, is so simple, so interesting, so suggestive, that a better condensation of Scriptural knowledge will never be written; and the marvel is that such a little miracle of instruction should have been laid aside by teachers."

It is striking that of all his written works apart from his hymns, his Divine Songs have been the most popular, but few have heard of his philosophical works! Tributes have been paid from other quarters that would have pleased Watts even more. A Christian periodical gave an account of the conversion of a young lady as a result of reading one of the verses of his "songs": "A poor wretched girl, religiously educated, but now abandoned to misery and want, with an illegitimate child, was struck with horror at hearing this infant daughter repeat, as soon as she could well speak, some of the profane language she had taught her by example. She trembled at the thought, that she was not only going to hell herself, but leading her child thither. She instantly resolved the first sixpence she could procure, should purchase Watts's Divine Songs, of which she had some recollection, to teach her infant daughter. She did so; and, on opening the book, her eye caught the following striking stanza:

'Just as the tree cut down, that falls
To north or southward, there it lies:
So man departs to heav'n or hell,
Fix'd in the state wherein he dies.'

She read on; the event ended in her conversion, and she lived and died a true child of God."

Castle and Mansion, Castle Hedingham

Let us now come to the "Songs" themselves. At various times Watts accompanied Sir Thomas and Lady Abney when they visited Mr. Robert Ashurst, of Hedingham Castle, Essex, a rich citizen, who had married Lady Abney's sister. While Watts was engaged upon his "Divine and Moral Songs," Mr. Ashurst was busy restoring, and practically rebuilding, his house, situated a short distance from the castle, and when he had discharged the workmen he invited the Abneys and Watts to pay him a visit. This was apparently in the spring of 1720, for in the Divine and Moral Songs, some of which were written at Hedingham Castle, we are taken in to the "meadows to see the young lambs" (Song 2); the tulips are in bloom and there is the reflection:

"How fair is the Rose! what a beautiful flower!
The glory of April and May;"

(Song 22)

(which reminds us that the seasons were in those days earlier than at the present time). It adds a new charm to these quaint but attractive Songs to recall that they were the result of saunterings in the old bird-haunted garden, among the hives, in "Dr. Watts's Walk," as his favourite sauntering place was later called, and under the beetling great keep of Hedingham.,[10] The pretty poem, "How doth the little busy bee," was probably not only a kindly message to children, but also a humorous compliment to the industry and taste displayed by Mr. Ashurst in restoring his house!

"How doth the little busy bee
Improve each shining hour,
And gather honey all the day
From every opening flower.
How skilfully she builds her cell!
How neat she spreads the wax!
And labours hard to store it well
With the sweet food she makes.
In works of labour, or of skill,
I would be busy too;
For Satan finds some mischief still
For idle hands to do.
In books, or work, or healthful play,
Let my first years be past,
That I may give for every day
Some good account at last."

In Song 22, "Against Pride in Clothes," verse 4 reads:

"The tulip and the butterfly
Appear in gayer clothes than I;
Let me be drest fine as I will
Flies, worms and flowers exceed me still."

He was in just the setting to compose such lines. In Song 30, on "innocent play," verse 2 reads:

"If we had been ducks we might dabble in mud,
Or dogs, we might play till it ended in blood:
So foul and so fierce are their natures.
But Thomas and William, and such pretty names
Should be cleanly and harmless as doves or as lambs,
Those lively, sweet, innocent creatures."

Thomas and William were something more than "two pretty names." They were the two brothers of Mr. Robert Ashurst, but as William was 24 and Thomas a little younger, there must have been some amusement when it was first read.

Watts may have been inspired by some of the workmen at Hedingham when he wrote:

"'Tis the voice of the sluggard; I heard him complain
You have waked me too soon, I must slumber again."

There is some evidence in his Songs of an indebtedness to John Mason. That Watts was indebted to others in the composing of his "Songs" is clear when we compare the lines of Bunyan's "Pismire" (Ant):

"Must we unto the pismire go to school,
To learn of her in summer to provide
For winter next ensuing? Man's a fool,
Or silly ants would not be made his guide.
But sluggard is it not a shame for thee
To be outdone by pismires?..."

with the following lines from Watts' "The Ant or Emmet":

"These Emmets, how little they are in our eyes!
We tread them to dust, and a troop of them dies,
Without our regard or concern:
Yet as wise as we are, if we went to their school,
There's many a sluggard, and many a fool,
Some lessons of wisdom might learn,"

It is highly probable that Watts, as he was constantly doing in his other works, took these poems from Bunyan and "improved" them.

Lewis Carroll

Perhaps the most striking proof of the popularity of his Songs can be seen from the fact that Lewis Carroll parodied some of his lines in "Alice in Wonderland." It can be safely assumed that the original was well known.

"How does the little busy bee
Improve each shining hour?"

becomes—

"How doth the little crocodile
Improve his shining tail?"

and

"'Tis the voice of the sluggard
I heard him complain,
You have waked me too soon,
I must slumber again."

becomes—

"'Tis the voice of the lobster
I heard him declare,
You have baked me too brown,
I must sugar my hair."

The gryphon knew the correct version. He had learned it at school!

Watts entered into the textbook field in 1721, when he published "The Art of Reading and Writing English." He dedicated this to the Abney girls, Sarah, Mary and Elizabeth. It was produced because he could find no spelling-book to meet his needs. He added that he had no intention of publishing it, but was urged to do so for use in a charity school sponsored by the Abneys at Cheshunt. On his title page occur the words:

"Let all the foreign tongues alone
'Til you can spell and read your own."

Watts's attitude was educationally unorthodox. Latin as the basis for all language instruction was firmly entrenched in the 18th century curriculum. Even in recent years Latin was regarded as essential to a correct study of English. Watts's industry was unbounded. We tend to think of him for his best-remembered works, his hymns and his children's songs, but he wrote many educational works. His "Logic," or "The Right Use of Reason in the Enquiry After Truth," was published in 1724. His aim was to give a "Variety of Rules to Guard Against ERROR in the Affairs of Religion and Human Life as well as in the Sciences." True logic was, for him, a practical science. Dr. Johnson paid a practical tribute to this work by including hundreds of examples and definitions in his Dictionary. It became a standard work at Oxford and Cambridge, and was popular in New England.

Astronomy

"The Knowledge of the Heavens and the Earth made Easy," or, the "First Principles of Astronomy and Geography," appeared in 1726. It, too, was written because Watts could find no "plain and easy" text on the subject. For its age and for its avowed purpose of introducing the study of astronomy to beginners, it was an excellent text. The outstanding feature of the work is its clarity. Knowing the value of a good recommendation, Watts, before publishing, sent the work for revision to John Eames, F.R.S., associate of Isaac Newton, and the best known scientist and science teacher among the Dissenters. Eames prefaced the text with the following note of commendation: "I think myself obliged in justice to the ingenious author as well as the public, to assure them that the alterations I have ventured to make in the revisal of this work, are but few and small. The same perspicuity of thought and ease of expression which distinguish his other works running thru the whole of this, I do not question but the world will meet with equal pleasure and satisfaction in the perusal."

Watts followed this work with a constant stream of publications. In 1728 he wrote, "Prayers Composed for Children"; "An Essay towards the Encouragement of Charity Schools" in 1729; Catechisms (1730); "A Brief Scheme of Ontology" (appended to Philosophical Essays, 1733); "Questions proper for Students in Divinity" (1740); "The Improvement of the Mind" Pt. I (1741)—Part II was published after his death in 1751—also a Discourse on the Education of Children and Youth, 1753.

These publications dealing with education, religious and secular, by no means tell the whole story. His Catechisms, for instance, each contain six items, each of which was published separately. There were many editions published both in England and America, and Watts's popularity continued past the middle of the 19th century. His views on education are particularly relevant today. In his discourse on the "Education of Children and Youth" he strikes a modern note. He writes of the "Exercise and Improvement of their natural powers," and says, "Almost everything is new to a child, and novelty will entice them onward to new acquisitions. Show them the birds, the beasts, the fishes, the insects, trees and herbs. Teach them to observe the various occurences in nature and providence, the sun, moon, and stars. The day and night, the hail, the snow, etc. You who instruct them should allure their young curiosity to ask many questions, and encourage them in it." Watts believed that the child had precious faculties that must be used to the full. Having a high view of God's creation and the dignity of man, he was anxious that the teacher should do justice to the child's latent powers. At the same time he knew that the child needed to be trained and was naturally lazy. He believed that man was a fallen creature, and that children must be under some constraint to work. However, he was wise in the use of compulsion. "The way to strengthen and improve the memory is to put it upon daily exercise. I do not mean that young children should be kept so close to their books as to be hammered with lessons all day long. The mind may be perplexed and confounded and the head overstrained and weakened. The powers of the mind as well as those of the body grow stronger by a constant and moderate exercise."

Watts was in an educational tradition that has enriched the life of this country. The Dissenting Academies played an important role in the development of modern education.

Dr. Johnson's praise of Watts's "Improvement of the Mind' helps us to see its origin in Watts's thinking: "Few books have been perused by me with greater pleasure than his Improvement of the Mind, of which the radical principles may indeed be found in Locke's 'Conduct of the Understanding,' but they are so expanded and ramified by Watts, as to confer upon him the merit of a work in the highest degree useful and pleasing. Whoever has the care of instructing others, may be charged with deficiency in his duty if this work is not recommended."

Watts's views on the question of recreation for the child were singularly broad for his day. The teacher should alternate play and study, but see to it that no jokes on sacred things or cruelty to animals be allowed. For the winter evenings, he disliked dice or cards, and, though he didn't speak himself against these pastimes, he was content for others to prove them unlawful.

Dr. Samuel Johnson from a portrait by Sir Joshua Reynolds

Yet he thought that more useful and instructive games could be played, and suggested card-games based on grammar, astronomy, and other subjects, all of which seems quite modern. (He would, doubtless, highly approve of "Scrabble.") He insisted that ghost stories, amorous romances, and the books of martyrs be kept away from younger children. The last, he believed, could frighten children. What would he have said of some television programmes young children are allowed to watch! In all instruction gentleness should rule and the hope of reward should be used rather than the fear of punishment. But he was strongly opposed to balls, masquerades, gaming-houses and the theatres. The student could learn the ways of the world safely through reading the Spectator instead of attending the theatre.

When considering the work of Watts as an educator, one needs to remember that he was influential first in guiding the educational work of his own denomination. The academies after 1690 were largely supported by boards composed of outstanding ministers within each denomination. Because of his position and because of his educational writings, he was generally accepted by his friends as the principal adviser on matters educational. Consequently, the Independents turned to him to choose and pass on tutors (as in the case of Doddridge). They also looked to him to recommend curricula for their schools and to supply texts.

The period of writing he covered (1705–1747) was one of England's most important literary eras. During these years the modern novel was born, the familiar essay under Addison and Steele developed into full maturity, and prose satire under Swift reached a height never equalled before or since. But these events seem to have passed over Watts as though he were in another age, and in one sense his prose works belonged to the previous century. His sermons and treatises of the popular religious type are eighteenth-century continuations of the work of Greenham, Rogers, Perkins, Goodwin, Baxter and other seventeenth-century Puritan divines.

He wrote many sermons. These were published as: A Sermon Preach'd at Salters' Hall, to the Societies for Reformation of Manners (1707), Sermons on Various Subjects, Divine and Moral. Vol. I (1720–1) Vol. II (1723) Vol. III (1729); Death and Heaven (1722) The Religious Improvement of Public Events (1727); A Collection of Sermons Preached at Bury Street by Several Ministers (1735); The World to Come, Part I (1739) Part II (1745) and Evangelical Discourses (1747). These sermons were written in the first place for his congregation at Bury Street, since from the year 1716, when he was restored from four years of sickness and confinement, his health had remained precarious, and frequent suffering considerably limited his public labours. For some time he had been often unable to preach, and when he did appear in the pulpit he was so weak afterwards that he had to go immediately to bed, and have his room in darkness and silence.

In such circumstances, to supply his lack of service he was encouraged to publish sermons that his people might read in their families those truths which they had heard with so much delight from his lips. One such volume is dedicated "To the Church of Christ assembling in Bury-Street," and dated at Theobalds, Feb. 21, 1721. "It often grieves me," he observes, "to think how poor, feeble, and short, are my present labours among you; and yet what days of faintness I generally feel after every such attempt, so that I am continually prevented in my design of successive visits to you, by the want of active spirits, while I tarry in the city; and yet if I attempt to stay a week or ten days there, I find a sensible return of weakness, so that I am constrained to retire to the country air." To be hindered from meeting his people in the sanctuary was a painful deprivation; but he had a place in their hearts, and experienced their kindest attentions. "I think," says he, "I can pronounce it with great sincerity, that there is no place, nor company, nor employment, on this side heaven, that can give me such a relish of delight, as when I stand ministering holy things in the midst of you. It is in the service of your souls, that I have spent the best period of my life, ministering the gospel among you. Two-and-twenty years are now expired since you first called me to this delightful work; and from that time my care and labours, my studies and prayers, have been employed in your behalf. I trust they have been accepted with God, and through his almighty blessing have obtained some success. As to their acceptance with you, I have too many and plain evidences to admit a doubt of it; which I have often thankfully acknowledged."

Watts was no malingerer. He really preferred to be with his people, as the above letter shows. Neither was he making excuses to get on with his studies, away from his responsibilities. In 1722 his health improved and so he preached again at Bury Street, but could not do this regularly, and so published sermons to make up for his absence. The reader may well be saying to himself, "What exactly was the matter with Watts?" The biographer has wondered, too. Clinical details were seldom given in biographies years ago. He appears to have had some nervous disorder which must have been aggravated by the way he drove his mind. He had such a love for study that he may have found it very hard to give his mind the rest it really needed.

His services to religion and literature were recognised widely, and in 1728 the Universities of Edinburgh and Aberdeen honoured him with a Doctorate of Divinity. "Academical honours," said Dr. Johnson, "would have more value if they were always bestowed with equal judgment."

At about this time Watts became the subject of attacks by a fellow-minister of a neighbouring Independent Church, Thomas Bradbury (referred to earlier), by reason of his statements regarding the Trinity. This subject deserves special attention since he has been similarly attacked ever since. We need, therefore, to make his position clear. Since the matter is complicated we have put his views in the Appendix (see Appendix III).

It is held by some that Watts's views on the Trinity underwent a change as a result of the debate on the subject that took place when certain West Country Presbyterian ministers were accused of Unitarianism. He tried to work out a scheme that would accommodate the rival parties, but in doing so became suspect of heresy himself. He tried to explain the unfathomable and made remarks that Bradbury and others used to imply ideas and views that he never held. At this time Watts had written his hymns, and his speculations had not entered them. He would have done well to have kept strictly to the attitude so well-expressed in his hymn on the Trinity:

"Almighty God to Thee
Be endless honours done;
The undivided Three
And the mysterious One.
Where reason fails with all her powers
There faith prevails and love adores."

Verse 4 No. 11.

Bradbury was a very different man from Watts. He was well-built with a strong voice, and always ready for controversy. He was nicknamed "make-a-noise Tom." He and Watts had been close friends, but Bradbury pursued him relentlessly on the question of the Trinity. In later years, the two happened to be together on the same platform and Watts found difficulty in making himself heard, because of his constitutional weakness. Bradbury called out, "Brother Watts, shall I speak for you?" The quiet little Doctor turned to him and said, "Why, Brother Bradbury, you have often spoken *against* me!"

Watts is to be remembered as an educator for his industry and for his devotion to an ideal. In the Preface of the "Rise and Progression of Religion in the Soul," Philip Doddridge, his protégé, evaluated Watts's services: "I congratulate you, dear sir, while you are in a multitude of families and schools of the lower class, condescending to the humble yet important work of forming infant minds to the first rudiments of religious knowledge and devout impressions, by your various catechisms and divine songs, you are also daily reading lectures of logic and other useful branches of philosophy to studious youth; and this not only in private academies but in the most public and celebrated seats of learning, not merely in Scotland, and in our American colonies, . . . but, through the amiable candour of some excellent men and accomplished tutors, in our English university. I too congratulate you that you are teaching no doubt hundreds of ministers and private Christians by your sermons, and other theological tracts, so happily calculated to diffuse through their minds that light of knowledge, and through their hearts that fervour of piety, which God has been pleased to enkindle in your own. But above all, I congratulate you that by your sacred poetry, especially by your psalms and your hymns, you are leading the worship, and, I trust also, animating the devotions of myriads in our public assemblies every Sabbath, and in their families and closets every day... Every word which you drop from the pulpit has now surely its peculiar weight. The eyes of many are on their ascending prophet eagerly intent that they may catch if not his mantle, at least some divine sentence from his lips, which may long guide their ways and warm their hearts." John Wesley's journal contains many accounts of Christians repeating or singing Watts's hymns on their death-beds.

Southampton

To return to Southampton, in 1719 the meeting-house and adjoining land at Southampton, which had been leased by Watts's father to the church, was purchased for £150. It had originally been leased from him by Robert Thorner, as mentioned earlier. A few years later the old building was pulled down and a larger one built

The plaque at the rear of the Marks and Spencer's premises at Southampton

on the site. It was again later rebuilt and enlarged, but was destroyed during the last war (1940). A plaque at the rear of Marks and Spencer's is a reminder that it was built on the site of the historic church. After the building was destroyed the congregation joined with the St. Andrews Presbyterian Church at Brunswick Place (now the United Reformed Church). It has in its possession some interesting memorials to Isaac Watts. The Isaac Watts Memorial Church (United Reformed), Winchester Road, was erected with the War Damage money that was given as a result of the destruction of the Above Bar Congregational Church.

When the new chapel at Southampton was erected, the minister, the Rev. William Bolar, chose as his assistant a friend of Watts, the Rev. Henry Francis. After some eighteen months Francis was unhappy at Southampton and thought of moving. Before he took the step, however, he wrote to Watts who, on 19th March, 1729, replied:

"Dear Brother Francis, —Your last is now before me with all the long detail of discouragements which enumerate there. I own many of them to be just, and the future prospects of the Dissenting interest in Southampton, after the lives of some few persons, is somewhat unpleasing and afflictive, if we look merely to appearances. But I have a few things to offer which will in some measure, I hope, reconcile your thoughts to a long continuance among them. 1. Consider how great things God has done for the Dissenting interest in Southampton by your means... 2. There are some persons in whom God has begun a good work... by your means. Oh, do not think of forsaking them! 3. There is scarce any people in England who love their minister and honour and esteem him more than yours do you... 4. Where is the man who is better qualified for carrying on God's work in the town than you are? 5. If you leave, whither will you go? The case is the same in many places as it is with you and much worse. 6. Consider whether this be not a temptation thrown in your way to discourage you in your work. 7. Let us remember that we are not engaged in a work that depends all upon reasonings, and prospects and probabilities, and present appearances, but upon the hand and Spirit of God. If He will work, who shall hinder?

"Farewell, dear Brother: meditate on these things. Turn your thoughts to the objects which are more joyful, and the occasions you have for thankfulness. Praise and thanksgiving are springs to the soul and give it new activity." It is good to know that Francis followed Watts's advice in this letter, and that he for many years ministered to a steadily increasing congregation, who showed their appreciation of his services by offering him, after the death of Mr. Bolar, the sole charge of the church.

Watts was himself like the "busy bee" he commended in his Songs, that was ready to "improve the shining hour." Well did he imitate the "ant and emmet," whether in writing personal letters as above, or for the public at large. He ever sought to be a teacher and guide to all who sought his help, while he sought to follow the One who was his own Instructor.

"Through this vain world He guides our feet
And leads us to His heavenly seat;
His mercies ever shall endure
When this vain world shall be no more."

Verse 6 No. 7

St. Stephens, Walbrook, London (Sir Christopher Wren: 1672-78)

Chapter 9

Empty Pews.

We are used to the sight of empty pews and churches closing in the mid-20th century, but this was a disturbing picture in the early 18th century. We have referred earlier to the state of affairs within the Establishment but shall now deal with the Dissenters. It was the Presbyterians who were in the greatest trouble and who were most anxious to arrest the decline. Large numbers of them were becoming Unitarian and this was followed by a coldness and formality and eventually by a numerical decline in the congregation. By the end of the century the denomination had about disappeared.

It had been far the largest of the dissenting body (some 1800 out of the 2,000 ejected ministers were Presbyterian) but was shrinking rapidly. Three ministers of this denomination printed their complaints about the state of affairs and assumed that things were in general decline. They recommended an accommodation to the times and the merging of congregations. In many respects their remedies are modern, both in their recommendation and in their failure to improve the situation. Philip Doddridge answered them by pointing out that things were not as bad in his part of the country and that the old method of expounding Scripture was the best means of reviving the churches.

A Living Message

He insisted that nothing but the plain, experimental, and affectionate proclamation of the doctrines of the gospel can preserve a congregation from decay, or revive it in decline. It was only, however, in particular districts, that decreased numbers and diminished spirituality appeared: of one of the midland counties, Northamptonshire, Doddridge testifies (in 1730) "I know that in many of the congregations the number of Dissenters is greatly increased within these twenty years; and the interest continues so to flourish, that I am confident some of our honest people, who converse only in their own neighbourhood, will be surprised to hear of an inquiry into the causes of its decay."

Watts was very interested in this revival in the East Midlands. There is evidence that numbers of both Independent and Particular Baptist Churches were being founded in these counties. A revival of religion in Olney was due largely to the efforts of Doddridge and two other ministers, who, after re-opening the chapel, applied to Dr. Watts for further guidance. The love and veneration with which the chapellers of Northamptonshire and Buckinghamshire—poor men in smock frocks and hobnailed boots, and poor women in cloaks—regarded Watts is strikingly illustrated by a letter of Doddridge to Watts. "On Wednesday last," he says, "I was preaching in a barn to a pretty large assembly of plain country people at a village a few miles off. After a sermon we sang one of your hymns—"Give me the wings of faith to rise"—and in that part of the worship I had the satisfaction to observe tears in the eyes of several of the auditory, and after the service was over some of them told me that they were not able to sing, so deeply were their minds affected with it; and the clerk in particular told me that he could hardly utter the words of it . . . when one of the company said, "What if Dr. Watts should come down to Northampton?" another replied with remarkable warmth, "The very sight of him would be like an ordinance to me!"

Watts was disturbed about the state of affairs among the Presbyterians, and was also concerned that the other Dissenters might prosper and increase. In 1730 and in March, in the following year,

Dr. Watts published his "Humble Attempt towards the revival of practical religion among Christians." This treatise began with: an address to ministers, "Take heed to the ministry which thou hast received;" and an address to the people, "What do ye more than others." The former part was drawn up for the ordination of Mr. John Oakes, to the church at Cheshunt, November 12, 1729; but being prevented by illness from attending, he was requested to publish what he had intended to deliver: the latter part is the substance of several sermons preached at Bury Street. This publication obtained an unexpected notoriety, as it originated an able controversy over the principles of nonconformity. In exhorting the dissenting body to increased purity of life and more active exertion, Dr. Watts assumed the fact that they were more favoured with advantages for the cultivation of personal religion, than the members of the establishment—that they were not so much in danger of substituting the outward forms of religion for the power – that they were freed from the inventions of men and the imposition of human ceremonies in divine worship – that they were not confined to a perpetual repetition of set forms of prayer – that they had the choice of their own ministers—that the communion of their churches was kept more pure and free from the admission of scandalous and unworthy members, and from these considerations he argues their obligation to improvement in proportion to their privileges. Though the writer had no design whatever to provoke a controversy; though his aim was to expose the failings of the Dissenters rather than those of the dominant hierarchy, yet, as the positions which he assumed involved all the main points at issue between Dissenters and churchmen, it was hardly to be expected that they would be received by them in silence. In his preface he makes a very important commentary on the state of affairs in nonconformity. "Among the papers published last year, there hath been some enquiry made, whether there be any decay of the dissenting interest, and what may be supposed to have been the occasion of it. So far as I have searched into these matters, I have been informed that whatsoever decrease may have appeared in some places there hath been sensible advances in others."

Mixed Conditions of the Churches

Watts was in a good position to judge. It is important to notice the fact that *some* churches were *advancing*, because this is generally ignored. Upon a careful examination of the evidence it is simple to see what was happening. Those churches that were abandoning the doctrines of the gospel were going down, but those that were true to the gospel were increasing. On the whole the Dissenters *were growing*, in spite of the decay among the Presbyterians.[11]

We have included some extract from Watts's "Humble Attempt" in Appendix IV since this serves the purpose of illustrating Watts's views, that remained the same at the end of his life as in his youth, and his oneness with the Evangelical awakening. It also gives the lie to the notion that Dissent was almost dead spiritually. His comments are also relevant to our day, which has real similarities.

The empty pews in Presbyterian and Anglican churches were a cause for alarm. General Baptist churches were also in decay. The Quakers, too, were not what they were. Infidelity to Christian revelation was rampant and Deism banished God from his universe. Watts was, as ever, ready to rise to the occasion, and did so in a most forceful manner in his "Humble attempt."

Dr. Watts, though never in the possession of robust health, was now enjoying an interval of comparative vigour, one of the few bright and sunny periods that mark his often clouded career. He appears to have occupied his pulpit regularly during the year 1731, and his indefatigable mind was employed on the deistical controversy. In the same year his work on "The Strength and Weakness of Human Reason," appeared anonymously. In opposition to these views, the necessity of a divine revelation is ably argued and satisfactorily proved in Watts's treatise; deism is chased through its various subterfuges; and reason is shown, from the history of human thought, to be a weak and erring faculty, utterly inadequate to find out the mind and will of the Most High. A close look at history will show how little the unaided powers of the human mind have been able to discover of moral and religious truth. The possession of the greatest talents has been no security from the grossest errors; though endowed with the most transcendant mental qualities, men have still remained perplexed with doubt, involved in uncertainty, and degraded by superstition. Very few even of the wisest ancients came near to grasping the most important truths recognized now by natural religion; they were deluded by the most trifling fancies, "that which profiteth not."

Watts the Philosopher

A production of a different character, the "Philosophical Essays," with the "Scheme of Ontology," was published in June, 1732. Some of his ideas are evidently founded upon the doctrines of Descartes, whose Principia Dr. Watts attentively read whilst a student in the academy. He was in early life a disciple of the fanciful, yet ingenious French philosopher, adopting and expanding his doctrine of spirits, but resigning his system of the material world at the feet of Newton. Though an ardent admirer, Dr. Watts was not a servile follower of the great philosopher: indeed, one design of the philosophical essays is to point out his fallacies, correct his mistakes, and warn the unwary against the errors into which they might be led by a blind deference to his authority.

Justly does Dr. Johnson remark, "Whatever he took in hand was, by his incessant solicitude for souls, converted to theology. As piety predominated in his mind, it is diffused over his works: under his direction it may be truly said, philosophy is subservient to evangelical instruction; it is difficult to read a page without learning, or, at least, wishing to be better. The attention is caught by indirect instruction; and he that sat down only to reason, is on a sudden compelled to pray."

On the 2nd April, 1732, Dr. Watts preached a funeral sermon for Miss Sarah Abney, the eldest daughter of Sir Thomas. "Religion was her early care, a fear to offend God possessed and governed her thoughts and actions from her childhood, and heavenly things were her youthful choice. She had appeared for some years in the public profession of Christianity, and maintained the practice of godliness in the church and the world; but it began much more early in secret. Her beloved closet and her retiring hours were silent witnesses of her daily converse with God and her Saviour." Among her papers were found recollections of the sermons she had heard, and a journal of her religious experience. Watts's labours had not been in vain.

Defence of the Faith

He wrote a treatise on the "Sacrifice of Christ, and the Operations of the Spirit" which appeared probably in 1735 (as a presentation copy is acknowledged by Bishop Gibson in that year). Dr. Watts was grieved to see, as he remarks, "a new sort of Christianity" published and propagated, referring to the defection of his presbyterian brethren; some had already discarded the necessity of a Redeemer to atone, and a Sanctifier to renew; and had abandoned the peculiar truths of the gospel for the cold and cheerless dogmas of natural religion. His treatise is, therefore, an attempt to contend for the "faith delivered to the saints" and proclaimed with such success from the pulpits of the first nonconformists.

Watts had every reason to suppose that the gospel was still relevant, even in the age of enlightenment, for much was happening to confirm his views. Doddridge wrote to Watts of the response he was getting from a monthly lecture he was invited to give at a nearby town.

"We have found a very numerous auditory, and apprehend, by the most moderate calculation, it must amount to near five hundred people. A great many of these are churchmen, who express very high satisfaction in what they hear. The Dissenters seem all satisfied, many of them much pleased; on all these accounts we think it a desirable thing that the lecture should still be supported. We can truly say, we know not any lecture to which an exhibition is granted, where the auditory is so numerous, and the prospects of usefulness seem more encouraging. Nor are we without our hopes, that the continuance of this lecture may be the means of fixing a regular minister here at length, which would be a great satisfaction to us, as we hope it might greatly conduce to the advancement of the truth as it is in Jesus, and the glory of God in the salvation of souls. One thing more we take leave to add, that though our preaching here has been evidently in the Calvinistical strain, and we judged it prudent at our first appearance here to declare our sentiments very freely and expressly in that respect, yet we do not find it has given any disgust to those of our hearers who statedly attend at church."

It is not surprising that Whitefield should have received such a response not many years later when he visited these parts.

In a letter to a friend Watts puts his doctrinal position clearly as what may be described as that of a "Moderate Calvinist." Appendix II.

There was considerable anxiety among the higher clergy of the Church of England about the general state of affairs. In 1734 the Bishop of London acknowledged Watts's "Logic" and expressed his deep concern.

Lifeless Religion

"Good Sir,

Since I received the favour of your present it has become part of my Sunday's exercise, and I have now read it over with pleasure, and I hope not without profit. The new notion that has prevailed among us of late years, that the Christian religion is little more than a good system of morality, must in course draw on a disregard to spiritual exercises, which calls on all serious Christians to do all that is in their power to raise and keep alive a spirit of devotion and piety in this lukewarm and degenerate age.

I pray God to give a blessing to your labours in this way, and remain with great respect,

"Sir,

"Your faithful friend and servant."

Variety of Activities

The tendency of Watts's mind was towards a life of seclusion; this inclination was strengthened by his frequent ill-health; but when summoned to the post of duty, he never failed to tear himself from his beloved solitude, to meet the task before him. And when he was free from the attacks of his complaint, the duties that fell to him were many and arduous. Besides his regular ministry at Bury Street, he had an extensive correspondence at home and abroad to maintain;

he was closely involved in various activities among the Dissenters; in the concerns of New England he took a prominent part; and he was frequently called upon to take special services. In the midst of such a vocation, and a constant martyr to sickness, for him to produce such a number of important works, covering so wide a range of subjects, shows an industry and application rarely equalled. Dr. Watts was, happily, placed in circumstances conducive to his taste and genius: he had none of the anxieties of domestic life, with a large share of its comforts: the kind attentions of Lady Abney provided all he needed to continue his studies. Under her roof he pursued the "noiseless tenor of his way," a blessing to the family, the church, and to the world, repaying the care of his hostess with his prayers and counsels. In doing good he was truly "in labours more abundant."

The contribution Watts made to the life of the dissenting churches must have been enormous. He was not satisfied however with "the day of small things," though he did not despise it. He longed for an awakening that would affect the country at large and did all he could to promote it. He lived to see it in his closing years.

"Jesus shall reign where'er the sun
Does his successive journeys run;
His kingdom stretch from shore to shore,
Till moons shall wax and wane no more."

No. 1.

George Whitfield preaching at Moorfields, London

Chapter 10
Revival

In the summer of 1736 Watts heard with joy of an amazing revival in New England through the preaching of Jonathan Edwards. He had kept up close contact with leaders there. Most of the churches were Independent, since the Mayflower Pilgrims were themselves of this viewpoint. Watts acted as literary agent for some of their most prominent men. He sent books to Harvard and Yale, where they were highly valued. He collected money for missionary work among the Indians and found donors for Harvard. He acted as trustee for two of her funds and helped to select her textbooks and her professors. He also gave advice to New England's governors. His works were widely read, and Jonathan Edwards appreciated his writings while at Yale. He opposed Watts in some theological matters, but was pleased to give him details of the Revival that took place at Northampton, Mass. Dr. Watts and his friend Dr. John Guyse wrote a foreword to an account of this great work published in England in 1737. We shall give some quotations as they serve to tell us both about Watts and the Revival itself. It will also show us his concern to see a similar work in England, which began in the year following its publication.

"The friendly correspondence which we maintain with our brethren of New England, gives us now and then the pleasure of hearing some remarkable instances of divine grace in the conversion of sinners, and some eminent examples of piety in that American part of the world. But never did we hear or read, since the first ages of Christianity, any event of this kind so surprising as the present Narrative hath set before us . . . We are abundantly satisfied of the truth of this narrative, not only from the pious character of the writer, but from the concurrent testimony of many other persons in New England; *for this thing was not done in a corner*. There is a spot of ground, as we are here informed, wherein there are twelve or fourteen towns and villages, chiefly situate in New Hampshire, near the banks of the river of Connecticut, within the compass of thirty miles, wherein it pleased God, two years ago, to display his free and sovereign mercy in the conversion of a great multitude of souls in a short space of time, turning them from a formal, cold, and careless profession of Christianity, to the lively exercise of every Christian grace, and the powerful practice of our holy religion. The great God has seemed to act over again the miracle of Gideon's fleece, which was plentifully watered with the dew of heaven, while the rest of the earth round about it was dry, and had no such remarkable blessing.

There has been a great and just complaint for many years among the ministers and churches in Old England, and in New, that the work of conversion goes on very slowly, that the Spirit of God in his saving influences is much withdrawn from the ministrations of his word, and there are few that receive the report of the gospel, with any eminent success upon their hearts. But as the gospel is the same divine instrument of grace still, as ever it was in the days of the apostles, so our ascended Saviour now and then takes a special occasion to manifest the divinity of this gospel by a plentiful effusion of his Spirit where it is preached: then sinners are turned into saints in numbers, and there is a new face of things spread over a town or a country . . . .

Certainly it becomes us, who profess the religion of Christ, to take notice of such astonishing exercise of his power and mercy, and give him the glory which is due, when he begins to accomplish any of his promises concerning the latter days: and it gives us further encouragement to pray, and wait, and hope for the like display of his power in the midst of us. *The hand of God is not shortened that it cannot save*, but we have reason to fear that *our iniquities*, our coldness in religion, and the general carnality of our spirits, have raised a wall of separation between God and us: and we may add, the pride and perverse humour of infidelity, degeneracy, and apostasy from the Christian faith, which have of late years broken out amongst us, seem to have provoked the Spirit of Christ to absent himself much from our nation. "Return, O Lord, and visit thy churches."

From such blessed instances of the success of the gospel, as appear in this narrative, we may learn much of the way of the Spirit of God in his dealing with the souls of men, in order to convince sinners, and restore them to his favour and his image by Jesus Christ, his Son . . . . Wheresoever God works with power for salvation upon the minds of men, there will be some discoveries of a sense of sin, of the danger of the wrath of God, and the all-sufficiency of his Son Jesus, to relieve us under all our spiritual wants and distresses, and a hearty consent of soul to receive him in the various offices of grace, wherein he is set forth in the Holy Scriptures . . . . And if our readers had opportunity (as we have had) to peruse several of the sermons which were preached during this glorious season, we should find that it is the common plain doctrine of the Reformation God has been pleased to honour with such illustrious success . . . .

It is worthy of our observation, that this great and surprising work does not seem to have taken its rise from any sudden and distressing calamity of public terror that might universally impress the minds of a people. . . It is a blessed confirmation of the truth of this present work of grace, that the persons who were divinely wrought upon in this season continue still to profess serious religion, and to practise it without returning to their former follies . . . . May a plentiful effusion of the blessed Spirit, also, descend on the British Isles, and all their American plantations, to renew the face of religion there!"

Watts and Whitfield

Since Watts firmly believed that the state of affairs in England could not be improved by any superficial means, he was glad of the opportunity to make his point in no uncertain manner by bringing the whole account to the attention of the English public. But when a similar work began to take place in England he did not at first recognise it for what it was, because of its circumstances. Many people visited him at Abney Park (Newington), among them Count Zinzendorf. He was on his way to New England to see the work of God, and was himself greatly used. "He is a person of uncommon zeal and piety and of an evangelical spirit," Watts wrote later, commending him to a New England friend. George Whitefield visited him shortly after the great work God had given him to do had begun. "The Holy Spirit," he said, "is working in the 18th century as He worked in the first. It has fallen to me to fight for the doctrine of Regeneration as Luther had fought for that of Justification by Faith. I am a new man," he said excitedly. "The Holy Spirit has singled me out for a great work." Whitefield had already started his open-air preaching that was drawing thousands, and knew that something remarkable was happening. Watts needed to be convinced, however. "Are you sure," Watts inquired calmly, "that the impression is Divine? Let me warn you against the danger of delusion, and to guard against the irregularities and imprudences to which youth and zeal may lead you. Though I believe you are very sincere, and that you desire to do good to souls, yet I am not convinced of any extraordinary call you have to some parts of your conduct."

Whitefield was right in that he was to be a special instrument of God to do a great work, but he over-stated his case by comparing himself with Luther. Luther did, indeed, fight for the doctrine of "Justification by Faith," since few believed it in Germany when he began his great work. This was not true of the doctrine of Regeneration in England at this time, however. It was held nominally at least by the Church of England, and was declared plainly by the majority of the Dissenters.

Whitefield would not have appreciated this since he had little contact with the latter. Watts would have had little sympathy with Whitefield's sweeping statement since he had in 1730 insisted upon the very things that Whitefield was saying, in his "Humble Attempt." We shall give some quotations in the Appendix to make this clear (Appendix VI). There was much happening already amongst the Dissenters, and spiritual life was not lacking, but what *Whitefield* had begun to do was something quite new. It was not *what* was said that was novel and startling, but the *way* it was being said. Whitefield was preaching in the open air, and this was unheard of. It was not permitted for a non-conformist minister to do this, and for an *Anglican* minister to do this was extraordinary. Furthermore, it was the *boldness* and plainness with which he spoke that amazed people. The numbers that gathered to hear him must have been composed of many dissenters who were delighted to hear such preaching in the open air, which was not permitted to their own ministers. It was also a sight for the huge London mobs to take an interest in. The effect of Whitefield's preaching was enormous, and caused a great stir. He was greatly assisted by the Holy Spirit in this phenomenal work. There was a great debate about his preaching in ecclesiastical circles, and at first Watts was uncertain what to make of him. However, when asked what he thought of him, when in the company of several other ministers, he replied, "My opinion is that Whitefield does more good by his wild notes than we do with our set music."

In April, 1742, Watts wrote concerning Whitefield, "Tho' I do not fall in with him in all his conduct, yet I cannot but think him a man raised up by Providence in something of an uncommon way to awaken a stupid and ungodly world to a Sense of the important Affairs of Religion and Eternity. You may show these letters of mine to what persons you please, and let my opinion of Mr. Whitefield even notwithstanding all his Imprudences, be known where you think fit." But even so, on September 20th, 1743, Watts remonstrated with Doddridge for taking part in Whitefield's service at his Tabernacle: "I am sorry that, since your departure, I have had many questions asked me about your preaching or praying at the Tabernacle, and of sinking the character of a minister, and especially of a tutor among the Dissenters, so low thereby. I find many of your friends entertain this idea; but I can give no answer, not knowing how much you have been engaged there. I pray God to guard us from every temptation."

Watts's coolness towards Whitefield appears surprising. Was Whitefield not, as he said earlier, a man "raised up" by God? There is a suspicion of a highchurchmanship that the Dissenters were accustomed to charge the Anglicans with! It was "right and proper" to describe the Great Awakening in New England among Independent churches in glowing terms for all to marvel at; it was also appropriate to commend an Anglican who was being used so remarkably to friends privately, but publicly to identify himself with him as Doddridge had done was too much, alas! The lines had been drawn very clearly between Church and Dissent, and though Watts was on friendly terms with the higher clergy, and was of a gentle and tolerant spirit, he was unwilling to get too close to Anglicans officially. It is not surprising, though, if one remembers the general intolerance of the day, and we should not expect even Watts to escape altogether. Many of the Dissenters, though, gave Whitefield great support by attending his meetings. Many pulpits were opened when the Anglican churches were closed to him. Furthermore, "Whitefield's Tabernacle" was largely paid for by contributions from the Dissenters.

Watts's sympathy with Whitefield increased, and he had close contact with others involved in the Methodist movement, such as the Countess of Huntingdon. Watts's "Humble Attempt" was bearing fruit, though not from the direction he expected it. But he was not sectarian at heart and at length "rejoiced that the Gospel was preached," whether by Churchmen or Dissenters.

The Great Awakening continued and all denominations gained much by it. The only exception was that of the Presbyterians that continued its slide into Unitarianism before disappearing altogether. Some churches had been full, but most had contained little but empty pews. The change was very great and lasted until this present century. Wattt's part in this great work is not without significance. He did all that was in his power to prepare the way for it.

"Blessings abound where'er He reigns,
The prisoner leaps to lose his chains,
The weary find eternal rest
And all the sons of want are bless'd."

verse 4. No. 1.

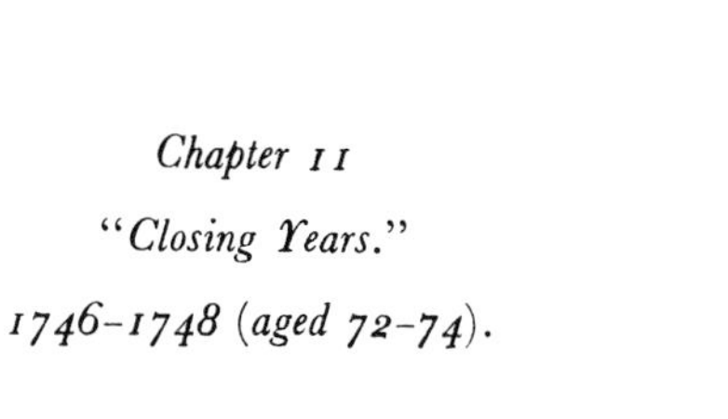

Chapter 11

"Closing Years."

1746–1748 (aged 72–74).

The domestic happiness which he had so long enjoyed, rarely disturbed except by the recurrence of ill-health, was interrupted from another quarter—the misconduct of some of his relatives—in the year 1746. This circumstance, whatever might be its nature, was very painfully felt: it destroyed for a time his balance: unused to such a trial, and in a state of great debility, his mind seems to have sunk for a time under the shock, and with difficulty to have recovered its balance. Lady Abney wisely kept the details of this unhappy affair from him. In August, while Watts was under the pressure of this calamity, Dr. Doddridge visited him and gives the following painful description of his aged friend—"His nephew, once so great a favourite, has done something to vex him, and his poor weak spirits cannot bear it; so that he is quite amazed, and even stupified with it to such a degree as hardly to take notice of anything about him; insomuch that, though he knew my chief reason of coming from Bath was to see him, he hardly took any notice of me; and instead of those tears and embraces with which he has often dismissed me, parted with me, though probably for the last time, as coldly as he did with young Mr. Lavington, who happened to be here, and who is entirely a stranger to him. This really astonished me and grieved me exceedingly." But the cloud that lowered in threatening blackness over his mind had been removed when in the February of the following year Mr. Barker wrote to Doddridge as follows:- "The behaviour of Dr. Richard Watts and the wretch Brackstone towards Dr. Isaac Watts, is a most marvellous, infamous, enormous wickedness.

Lady Abney, with inimitable steadiness and prudence, keeps her friend in peaceful ignorance, and his enemies at a becoming distance; so that in the midst of this cruel persecution of that righteous man, he lives comfortably; and when a friend asks him how he does, answers, "Waiting God's leave to die." That he sometimes felt impatience under his heavy afflictions, is but saying that he was human. "Sometimes," he said, "I have been ready to say within myself, "Why is my life prolonged in sorrow? Why are my days lengthened out to see further wretchedness? Methinks the grave should be ready for me and the house appointed for all the living. What can I do further for God or for men here on earth, since my nature pines away with painful sickness, my nerves are unstrung, my spirits dissipated, and my best powers of acting are enfeebled and almost lost? Peace, peace, O thou complaining spirit. Dost thou know the counsels of the Almighty, and the secret designs of thy God and thy Saviour? He has many deep and unknown purposes in continuing his children amidst heavy sorrows, which they can never penetrate or learn in this world. Silence and submission become thee at all times."

Strange Stories

Much misapprehension has existed with reference to the state of Dr. Watts's mind in his latter days. Stories of his strange nervous affections, his wild and extraordinary fancies, amounting to intellectual derangement, have been circulated. "How it came to pass," says Dr. Gibbons, "I know not, but that it has so happened is certain, that reports have been raised, propagated, and currently believed, concerning the Doctor, that he has imagined such things concerning himself, as would prove, if they were true, that he sometimes lost possession of himself, or suffered a momentary eclipse of his intellectual faculties. But I take upon me, and feel myself happy to aver, that these reports were utterly and absolutely false and groundless; and I do this from my own knowledge and observation of him for several years, and some of them the years of his decay, when he was at the weakest; from the express declaration of Mr. Joseph Parker, his amanuensis for above twenty years, and who was in a manner ever with him; and above all from that of Mrs. Elizabeth Abney, the surviving daughter of Sir Thomas and Lady Abney, who lived in the same family with him all the time of the Doctor's residence there, a period of no less than thirty-six years. Can any evidence be more decisive?"

The volume of "Evangelical Discourses" appeared at the beginning of 1747 with an "Essay on the Powers and Contests of Flesh and Spirit" added to it. This is dedicated to the church in Bury Street, and may be regarded as their pastor's farewell benediction. Among his affectionate advice on an occasion so solemn he says "Continue to be of one mind: live in peace: be careful to practice all the duties of holiness and righteousness: keep close to God by humble fervent prayer and dependence; seek his face for direction, and a blessing in all your affairs." He acknowledges with gratitude the great harmony which had existed for more than forty-three years between him and his worthy colleague, Mr. Price, and with complete confidence resigns his change entirely to his care. "There," he remarks, speaking of "that blessed book" from which he had so often discoursed to them, "all my hopes of eternal life are fixed, and in this hope I trust all of you will be found walking steadfastly in the same faith, by the same rule, till you are at length made happy partakers of the same salvation."

Thus one year and eight months before his death Dr. Watts terminated the toils of authorship. His time was now spent in devotional exercises, occasional correspondence, arranging his papers, and receiving the visits of a few of his closest friends. The Right Hon. Arthur Onslow, Speaker of the House of Commons, who was on friendly terms with the leading dissenting ministers sought an interview with him at this time. Dr. Gibbons relates this incident, honourable to both men as follows: "Not long before his death, he made a visit to Dr. Watts at Stoke Newington, for the purpose of gratifying himself with the sight of so great and good a man, whom he held in the highest esteem, and, I might truly say, above the common rank of mortals. The Speaker declared to me, that when he saw him he thought he saw a man of God."

Mr. Onslow was not the only "Speaker" to pay tribute to Isaac Watts! The last months of his life were of prolonged sickness and mental weakness. It was a sore trial for one whose mind had been so active. We are indebted to Dr. Gibbons for details of his conduct at such a time. There is no doubt that there is some hero-worship with Dr. Gibbons but we must take his words seriously.

"I never could discover," says Dr. Gibbons, "though I was frequently with him, the least shadow of a doubt as to his future everlasting happiness, or anything that looked like an unwillingness to die. How have I known him recite with a self-application those words in Hebrews 10, v 36 "Ye have need of patience, that after ye have done the will of God ye may receive the promise!" And how have I heard him, upon leaving the family after supper and withdrawing to rest, declare with the sweetest composure, that if his Master were to say to him he had no more work for him to do, he should be glad to be dismissed that night!

"When he was almost worn out and broken down by his infirmities he observed, in conversation with a friend, that he re membered an aged minister used to say, that the most learned and knowing Christians, when they come to die, have only the same plain promises of the gospel for their support, as the common and unlearned; "And so," said he, "I find it. They are the plain promises of the gospel which are my support, and I bless God they are plain promises, which do not require much labour or pains to understand them; for I can do nothing now but look into my Bible for some promise to support me, and live upon that."

On Friday, November 25th in the afternoon, aged seventy-four years, Dr. Watts bade farewell and peacefully resigned his spirit into the hands of his Lord and Saviour. He directed in his will that his remains should be interred in Bunhill Fields, among many of his pious fathers and brethren, whom he had known in the flesh, and with whom he wished to be found in the resurrection. To show his catholic spirit he desired that his funeral should be attended by two Independent ministers, two Presbyterian, and two Baptist.

On Monday, December 5th, the body was laid in its final resting-place, in the presence of an immense number of people.

Dr. Watts composed his own humble epitaph.

"Isaac Watts, D.D. pastor of a church of Christ in London, successor to the Rev. Mr. Joseph Caryl, Dr. John Owen, Mr. David Clarkson, and Dr. Isaac Chauncey, after fifty years of feeble labours in the gospel, interrupted by four years of tiresome sickness, was at last dismissed to his rest—

"In uno IESU omnia

"2 Cor. v8 Absent from the body, and present with the Lord."
Watts's will shows first of all that, though not a rich man, he died well beyond the reach of poverty. He left bequests amounting to approximately £2,900, exclusive of his books, his household effects, and his copyrights on works. This sum includes only actual money and stocks. Watts's will is, moreover, eloquent testimony to his tolerance. He left money not only to poor dissenting preachers but also to the poor of the Established Church in Southampton.

"I'll praise my Maker with my breath,
And when my voice is lost in death,
Praise shall employ my nobler powers:
My days of praise shall ne'er be past,
While life, and thought, and being last,
Or immortality endures," No. 8.

Chapter 12
Isaac Watts Today

The memory of Isaac Watts has been preserved for us by a statue in Southampton, a bust in Westminster Abbey, and some seven portraits, besides his innumerable written works. The statue in Southampton deserves special mention. It stands in the Western Park (also known as Watts's Park), and is of white Sicilian marble. It surmounts a pedestal of polished grey Aberdeen granite, which has three basso-relievos on the sides. On the south side (front) Watts is represented instructing a group of children, while below is the inscription: "He gave to lisping infancy its earliest and purest lessons."

On the west side he is sculptured with upturned glance; and underneath is his own descriptive line, "To heaven I lift my waiting eyes." On the east side he is depicted as a philosopher, with globe, telescope and hour-glass; illustrating Johnson's observation, "He taught the art of reasoning, and the science of the stars."

On the north side is a marble tablet inscribed:

A.D. 1861
ERECTED BY VOLUNTARY SUBSCRIPTIONS
IN MEMORY OF ISAAC WATTS, D.D.,
A NATIVE OF SOUTHAMPTON.
BORN 1674, DIED 1748.

"From all that dwell below the skies,
Let the Creator's praise arise;
Let the Redeemer's name be sung
Through every land, by every tongue."

Watts (Psalm cxvii)

It is fitting that the verse chosen for the monument should have been from Psalm 117. It well expresses Watts's ardent desire that his

Lord and Saviour should have the utmost praise. It was the sole object to which he directed all his great endeavours.

There have been a number of occasions when celebrations have been held in Southampton to his memory. There was the bicentenary of his birth in 1874, when civic celebrations were held. In 1901 he was remembered in connection with the Congregational 20th Century Fund. Again, in 1948, Southampton remembered him with the bicentenary of his death. The Tudor House Museum has some interesting items in it connected with him. It contains a photo of the back of 41, French Street, and a painting of the front of it. It is the home of the latest painting of Dr. Watts, undertaken by Gordon Fry,[12] copied from the National Portrait Gallery painting by Sir Godfrey Kneller. The front cover of this book is from a photograph of Kneller's portrait. Sir Godfrey Kneller was Principal Painter to the court of Charles II, and painted contemporary figures such as Sir Isaac Newton and Sir Christopher Wren. The most "striking" memorial to Watts, however, has been provided by the Civic Centre clock, Southampton. Every four hours (in the daytime), starting at 8.00 a.m., the clock sounds out the notes of "St. Anne," the familiar tune that traditionally accompanies "O God, our help in ages past . . . ." The local radio station, Radio Solent, also regularly makes use of its first few notes. He has become, clearly, Southampton's most remembered son. Dr. Johnson's appreciation of the man was comprehensive: "Few men have left behind such purity of character or such monuments of laborious piety. He has provided instruction for all ages, from those who are lisping their first lessons to the enlightened readers of Malbranche and Locke; he had left neither corporal nor spiritual natures unexamined; he has taught the art of reasoning and the science of the stars. His character, therefore, must be formed from the multiplicity and diversity of his attainments, rather than from any single performance; for it would not be safe to claim for him the highest rank in any single denomination of literary dignity; yet perhaps there was nothing in which he would not have excelled, if he had not divided his powers to different pursuits."

Having heard such tributes are we to leave the matter there and remind ourselves that it is 300 years since he was born?

We have looked back and been absorbed with the genius of a man who for two centuries had a considerable influence not only in this country, but abroad. His books were published far and wide for many years after his death. But though scores of his hymns are still sung, there is a vast difference between the popularity he enjoyed even at the beginning of this century, and the present time. Has he little, therefore, to say to us? Should our interest in him, therefore, be purely of antiquarian nature? We have much to learn from him in three fields, those of education, worship and spiritual revival.

We can still learn from the gentle Dr. Watts, who was ever willing to impart his wisdom.

Education

Modern educationalists can find much to interest them in Watts because he was a pioneer in this field. He was not alone, but shared in the great contribution to education that was made by the Dissenters, and that goes back to John Calvin and the Reformation. This matter is dealt with in depth by Ashley Smith in his "The Birth of Modern Education—the Contribution of the Dissenting Academies" 1660–1800 (Independent Press 1954). In the light of the present debate on education Watts and his contemporaries have much to say to modern educationalists. He was influenced by John Locke in his understanding of the purpose of education as the means of equipping men to discover themselves and to create their own institutions. Believing, as he did, that man was a "fallen" creature, spiritually dead and in need of regeneration, he nevertheless believed that there remained in him many wonderful propensities that should be cultivated, stimulated and harnessed. He did not believe that sin had corrupted the *mechanism* of the body, but rather inclined men to *use* their faculties wrongly. Consequently, he believed that the body and mind should not be handled oppressively, and simply shaped for institutional goals. On the other hand he believed that unbridled self-expression could be ruinous since man's nature was basically selfish. A measure of compulsion was necessary, therefore. It has been said that in him we see the humanism of the Renaissance and the Calvinism of the Puritans combined. He would have simply attributed his views to a Biblical view of human nature. Man was more than a piece of wood or stone to be chiselled into shape, since he has been "wonderfully made." All his natural gifts must, therefore, be given the proper opportunity to develop, and can be damaged by a wrong approach. The very title of his great work, "The Improvement of the Mind," is eloquent of his approach. The faculties must be developed, but at the same time put to good use. Men do not naturally always want what is good for them, nor for others. There is much for modern educationalists to admire in Watts. I hope I have aroused some curiosity!

Worship

His hymns are still sung by millions the world over. The words of the familiar, "Jesus shall reign . . .", which continue:

> "People and realms of every tongue
> Dwell on His love with sweetest song"

have been amply fulfilled since his day, and it is remarkable that it is often Watts's words that they are singing. He is still popular. This is no mean achievement. He was popular without being cheap. To him the praise of God was the highest exercise man could perform. He was equipped in every way, as we have seen, to be the pioneer and "Father of the modern hymn." He excelled most in those that are taken up with sheer praise.

"Join all the glorious names
Of wisdom, love and power,
That ever mortals knew,
That angels ever bore;
All are too mean to speak His worth,
Too mean to set my Saviour forth."

Whilst it is true that Charles Wesley's hymns are sung about as much as Watts's, there are certain factors that put Watts ahead, in my opinion. Wesley's themes were more limited than those of Watts, and only a fraction of his 6,500 hymns are still sung. A far larger proportion of Watts's 700 are still with us after 250 years.

Watts saw hymn-singing as an offering to God, above everything else. He had a high view of God, and so His praise must be worthy. He lived in a day when the praise of God was dull and dreary. There was the "fear of the Lord," the awe and respect of God, but praise was a burden because of its form. Watts was anxious to make it a joy to the senses. "Religion never was designed to make our pleasure less." Today, alas, the opposite is the case. There has been a swing to the other extreme. Worship has become entertainment. In the desire to attract people to empty churches, and to popularise Christianity, it has been cheapened. We are going back to the Middle Ages when every device imaginable was used to popularise Christianity, and the effect then was to alter the message, and lose its power. To Watts, the Word of God is our guide. God Himself has prescribed the way we should approach Him. The Old Testament contains very careful instructions, and the New Testament contains directions that are to be followed with equal care. He was no innovator, but a Reformer, and was anxious to take people back to the New Testament. He would have been horrified at many of the lyrics and the accompanying tunes that are offered to God in praise and worship so often today. For many it is a question of entertainment rather than worship.

It was his theology that made him think as he did:

"Before Jehovah's aweful throne
Ye nations bow with sacred joy.
Know that the Lord is God indeed;
He can create and He destroy."

There was indeed joy for him in worship, but it was a *sacred* joy. He knew the joy of a genuine Christian experience, and his paraphrase of Ephesians 3:16 etc. exhibits this:

"Come, dearest Lord, descend and dwell
By faith and love in ev'ry breast.
Then shall we know and taste and feel
The joys that cannot be expressed."

He did not have to resort to sentimental words and sloppy tunes to express a deep experience of the love of God.

If I have succeeded in producing in the reader a greater appreciation of the hymns we still sing that Watts wrote, I shall have fulfilled the main purpose of this memorial. One day, before devoting a day to work on this book, I read Psalm 89:7 and was greatly struck by its relevance: "God is greatly to be feared in the assembly of the saints and to be had in reverence of all them that are about Him." Watts teaches us to do this very thing, without making worship a burden. We live in days when man is deified and God humanised.

Revival

Finally, we can learn much from a comparison between our day and Watts'. He looked for the day when the churches would be filled once more and the people of God revived, and he was not disappointed. But he did not passively wait for it to happen. Even before the outstanding ministry of George Whitefield began much had been going on. Indeed, there was a continual witness to the reality of the Gospel in many of the dissenting congregations, though little notice was taken of it then, nor has been since. Through his labours he helped keep this witness alive, and prepared the way for greater things. Is there not a lesson here for today? God is able to repeat his "Wonders of Grace" and do what he did in the 18th century in the 20th. But he also did much to encourage those who were faithfully persevering amidst much opposition. There are many today similar to those in Watts's day that still maintain a faithful witness. May they look to the One who can do "beyond all we can ask or think" and, at the same time, follow Watts's example of the diligent use of every talent. We may not aspire to his gifts, but should surely be motivated by the same high aims.

"Were the whole realm of Nature mine
That were an offering far too small;
Love so amazing, so divine
Demands my soul, my life, my all."

verse 4. No. 9.

Notes

(1) Some have queried the traditional site of the imprisonment.
(2) Paxton Hood: "Life of Watts" p. 9.
(3) Independent churches generally followed the 'congregational' principle of deciding all matters at the church meeting when everyone could take part. This was the practise of the "Mayflower Pilgrims". Hence the term Independent was gradually superceded by the term 'Congregational'.
(4) There is some doubt about the place of Watts' birth. Traditionally it is 41, French Street, but in 1927 Dr. J. W. Horrocks threw doubt on this because Watts was born "without the Bar". The existence of 41, French Street in Watts' day is also in doubt. However, there is no doubt that this marks the site of a residence of the Watts family.
(5) Those churches in Russia that will not "register" (and this involves some vital principles) suffer in a manner remarkably similar to these outlined, in terms of a scale of fines, imprisonment and exile to Siberia, according to repeated offences. Many today are separated from their families as Isaac Watts, senior, was. The State believes that their independence constitutes a political threat, justs as it did in 17th century England.
(6) The length of the service may seem very drawn out to us. In Russia today this is a common practice among those meeting secretly. They value the opportunity once they get it!
(7) Thorner became a benefactor of Harvard. "Thorner's Homes" are still in existence in Southampton today. Some new homes were opened at Regent's Park as recently as 1971, as part of a redevelopment scheme, and accommodation for 169 provided at Henstead Road. Through the charity of R. Thorner, hundreds of widows have been able to enjoy quietness and security for many years.
(8) These two important entries were omitted from the memoranda without explanation in the 1901 Watts Commemoration in connection with the Congregational "20th Century Fund". They were, however, included in the 1948 bi-centenary Civic celebrations. They are authentic, and indicate that Watts' experience was typical of many in his day. Only 12 years earlier Bunyan, in his "Pilgrim's Progress", set forth a pattern of the Christian experience in which Christian bore his burden for some time before gaining relief at the cross.
(9) Abney House. Typical of the type of house fully established by 1685–90. It illustrates the Dutch influence arising in England from association with Holland in the latter half of the seventeenth century. It is typical of houses designed by Sir Christopher Wren (1632–1723) and his contempories.
(10) Hedingham Castle provides a good example of a norman square tower keep (circa 1140).
(11) Because it is an almost universal assumption that Dissent was generally in decay before the Evangelical Awakening the reader is invited to consult the "History of the Dissenters" (1681–1808) by Bennett and Bogue. These four volumes are very rare, but are extremely thorough. They demonstrate beyond doubt that Dissent was strongly advancing all through Watts's life, though it was largely due to the increase among Independents and Particular Baptists. See also my treatise on "The Forgotten Baptists" 1660–1760, published by the same publisher as this volume.
(12) This portrait was commissioned by Marks & Spencers Ltd. to be displayed by them on the site of the Old Above Bar Church until given to the City to be permanently displayed in the Tudor House Museum.

Select Bibliography

Memoirs of Isaac Watts, by Dr. Thomas Gibbons.
Isaac Watts, his life and Writings, by E. Paxton Hood.
Life Times and Correspondence of Isaac Watts, by Thomas Milner.
Life of Isaac Watts, Thomas Wright.
Isaac Watts, his life and Works, Arthur Paul Davis.
These are all out of print. A more recent study of Watts as a hymnwriter is still available; Isaac Watts, Hymnographer, Harvey Escott. Independent Press.
This is a very thorough and sympathetic study.

APPENDIX I

In a letter to his brother Enoch he outlines the difference between the various opinions held in his day. The comments are most instructive. We shall, however, restrict the statement to his description of those he had closest association with doctrinally, namely the Baptists and Independents.

"The Baptists differ not from Calvinists in their doctrine, unless in the article of infant baptism; they generally deny any children to be in the covenant of grace, and so deny the seal of the covenant to them. They deny baptism by sprinkling to be real and true baptism. In church government they are Independents". The Baptist churches apart from the Arminian Baptists differed little from Watts on matters of both faith and order. Concerning "Independents", he wrote:

"There were some of the Independents heretofore called Brownists, some of whom were very irregular in the management of church affairs, but they are not to be found now: the tenets of rigid Independents are: 1st. That every church hath all the power of governing itself in itself, and that everything done in a church must be by the majority of the votes of the brethren. 2nd. That every church has its minister ordained to itself, and that he cannot administer the ordinances to any other people, and if he preaches among others it is but as a gifted brother. But the generality of Independents follow rather Dr. Owen's notions; their tenets are such as these: 1st. That the power of church government resides in the pastors and elders of every particular church, and that it is the duty of the people to consent. 3rd. They generally think a minister not to be ordained but to a particular church though many of them now think that, by virtue of communion of churches, he may preach authoritatively, and administer the ordinances to other churches upon extraordinary occasions. 4th. That it is not absolutely necessary that a minister be ordained by the imposition of hands of the other ministers, but only requisite that other ministers should be there present as advisers and assistants when he is ordained by the church; that is, set apart by their choice and his acceptance. 5th. They generally hold more to the doctrine of Calvin than Presbyterians do. 6th. They think it not sufficient ground to be admitted a member, if the person be only examined as to his doctrinal knowledge and sobriety of conversation; but they require with all some hints, or means, or evidences of the work of grace on their souls, to be professed by them, and that not only to the minister but to the elders also, who are joint rulers in the church. 7th. They do not require (as some think) a word of scripture, or time, or place, or sermon, by which they were converted; for very few can tell this; but only they discourse and examine them a little of the way of their conviction of sin, of their being brought to know Christ; or at least ask them what evidences they can give why they hope they are true believers, and try to search whether there be sincerity in the heart, as much as may be found by outward profession, that they may, as much as in them lies, exclude hypocrites".

APPENDIX II

"Sir,

"Your letter, dated about the middle of October, should have been answered long ago, had I not been withheld from my study by long illness; nor am I yet fully recovered. I take pleasure, Sir, to find your honest inquiries after truth, and that you are not willing either to put off your children, or to be contented yourself, with a mere set of words, instead of clear and intelligible doctrines.

"I will, therefore, write you my thoughts in a few lines, of that impotency and inability of man to believe and repent, and return to God, which arises from the fall, and which is, I think, the best and the only way to secure our thoughts from running into the extremes of Antinomian opinions on the one side, or Arminian on the other.

"This impotency, though it may be called natural, or rather, native, as it comes to us by nature in its present corrupted state, yet it is not a want of natural powers, either of understanding or will, to know or choose that which is good; for if there were not natural powers sufficient for this purpose, I do not see men could be charged as criminals, in not receiving the gracious offers of the gospel. This impotence, therefore, is what our divines usually call a moral impotence, i.e. their mind will not learn divine things, because they shut their eyes; they will refuse the proposals of grace, they shut it out of their hearts, they have a delight in sin, and dislike to Christ and his salvation; they have a rooted obstinacy of will against the methods of divine mercy, and against the holiness which is connected with happiness. And yet this moral impotency is described in scripture by such methods as represent us "blind", or "dead in sin", and that we can no more change our nature, than the Ethiopian can change his skin, or the leopard his spots; and the reason of these strong expressions is, because God knows this natural aversion to grace and holiness is so strong and rooted in their hearts, that they will never renounce sin and receive the salvation of Christ, without the powerful influence of the Spirit of God, even that same Spirit which can cure those who are naturally blind, or can raise the dead.

"Now, that this weakness of man to do that which is good is a moral impotence, appears by the moral remedies which are applied to cure it; viz. commands, promises, threatenings, which sort of methods would be useless and ridiculous to apply to natural impotence; that is, to make the blind see, or the dead arise. It must be concluded, therefore, that man had a natural ability, i.e. natural powers, to do what God requires, but at the same time such a native aversion of will, that he will never do it without divine grace. Thus there is a fair way laid for the necessity of divine grace, and yet at the same time a just foundation laid for the condemnation of impenitent sinners".

He well knew the important distinction made between moral and physical ability. Jonathan Edwards may well have confirmed his views in this direction.

APPENDIX III

In 1726 he wrote to Bradbury, "You tell me that the plain drift of this whole imagination of resembling the being of God by the soul of man, is to destroy a Trinity of Persons". (Watts had done this earlier, and had suggested that Christ had a human soul before the incarnation.) "Now I have often freely declared, and still declare, that I allow the greatest distinction possible between the sacred Three in the divine nature, which does not arise to three distinct conscious minds or spirits. Make it as great as you will short of this, and I acquiese in it. But, then, since three distinct conscious minds is the true idea of three proper literal persons, whatsoever falls short of this can be but an analogical personality; yet if any man will call this a proper divine personality, though it is but similar to human personality, I will not contend about words and names. And whereas I have sometimes called the Word and Spirit, in the divine nature, two distinct powers or principles of operation in the godhead, yet I have in many places told what I mean, viz. that the idea of distinct powers or principles of operation, being the greatest distinction that we can conceive in one spirit, it is the nearest analogical idea of the sacred Three that I can arrive at, always supposing there may be some unknown distinction in the divine nature greater than the ideas we have of the powers or faculties in the soul of man. If I have either given you or any one else occasion to understand me in a different sense from what I now declare, I should be glad to retrieve any such mistake of my meaning. It has always been a painful and grievious thing to me, to hold a contest with any person living, much more with one for whom I have had so sincere an esteem, more especially since my constitution and my spirits are much broken by my illness. If, therefore, the temper of your mind continues the same as runs through a good part of your two letters to the board and me, I can neither desire nor expect a return to this paper; nor am I willing by any means to carry on such an epistolary contention. If you think fit to talk with me on any of these heads, in a spirit of meekness, I am very ready to give you further satisfaction about any of them."—"Let us examine concerning what is past, and let us take care for the time to come, that what we write or print with regard to our brethren, be expressed in such language as may dare appear and be read by the light of the last conflagration, and the splendour of the tribunal of our returning Lord."

He affirmed that he was well satisfied in the general doctrine, "that true and proper Godhead is ascribed to our Lord Jesus Christ and the Holy Spirit in many places of scripture". He was no Unitarian. Basically he believed in the Trinity, but was not sure that the Athanasian Creed was the best way of expressing it.

APPENDIX IV

I. In choosing your texts, or themes of discourse, *seek such as are most suited to do good to souls,* according to the present wants, dangers, and circumstances of the people; whether for the instruction of the ignorant; for the conviction of the stupid and senseless; for the melting and softening of the obstinate; for the conversion of the wicked; for the edification of converts; for the comfort of timorous and mournful; for gentle admonition of backsliders, or more severe reproof. Some acquaintance with the general case and character of your hearers is needful for this end.

II. In handling the text, divide, explain, illustrate, prove, convince, infer, and apply in such a manner, as to do real service to men, and honour to our Lord Jesus Christ. Do not say within yourself, How much or how elegantly I can talk upon such a text, but what can I say most usefully to those who hear me, for the instruction of their minds, for the conviction of their consciences, and for the persuasion of their hearts? Be not fond of displaying your learned criticisms in clearing up the terms and phrases of a text, where scholars only can be edified by them; nor spend away the precious moments of the congregation, in making them hear you explain what is clear enough before, and hath no need of explaining; nor in proving that which is so obvious that it wants no proof. This is little better than trifling with God and man. Think not, How can I make a sermon soonest and easiest? but how I can make the most profitable sermon for my hearers; not what fine things I can say, either in a way of criticism or philosophy, or in a way of oratory and harangue, but what powerful words I can speak to impress the consciences of them that hear with a serious and lasting sense of moral, divine, and eternal things. Judge wisely what to leave out as well as what to speak. Let not your chief design be to work up a sheet, or to hold out an hour, but to save a soul.

III. In speaking of the great things of God and religion, remember you are a minister of Christ and the gospel, sent to publish to men what God has revealed by his prophets and apostles, and by his Son Jesus; and not a heathen philosopher to teach the people merely what the light of reason can search out: Your are not to stand up here as a professor of ancient or modern philosophy, nor an usher in the school of Plato or Seneca, or Mr. Locke; but as a teacher in the school of Christ, as a preacher of the New Testament. You are not a jewish priest, to instruct men in the precise niceties of ancient judaisms, legal rites and ceremonies; but you are a christian minister; let christianity, therefore, run through all your composures, and spread its glories over them all.

It is granted, indeed, that reasonings from the light of nature have a considerable use in the ministry of the gospel. It is by the principles of natural religion, and by reasoning from them on the wonderful events of prophecy and miracle, etc., that we ourselves must learn the truth of the christian religion, and we must teach the people to build their faith of the gospel on just and rational grounds; and this may perhaps, at some time or other, require a few whole discourses on some of the principal themes of natural religion, in order to introduce and display the religion of Jesus.

But such occasions will but seldom arise in the course of your ministry. It is granted also, that it is a very useful labour sometimes in a sermon, to shew how far the light of nature and reason will carry us on in the search of duty and happiness; and then to manifest how happily the light of scripture supplies the deficiencies of it; that the people may know how greatly they are indebted to the peculiar favour of God for the book of divine revelation.

If you speak of the duties which men oew to God, or to one another, even those which are found out by reason and natural conscience, shew how the gospel of Christ hath advanced and refined every thing that nature and reason teach us: Enforce these duties by motives of christianity, as well as by philosophical arguments drawn from the nature of things: Stir up the practice of them by the examples of Christ and his apostles, by that heaven and that hell which are revealed to the world by Jesus Christ our Saviour: Impress them on the heart by the constraining influence of the mercy of God and the dying love of our Lord Jesus Christ, by his glorious appearance to judge the living and the dead, and by our blessed hope of attending him on that day. These are the appointed arguments of our holy religion, and may expect more divine success.

If you would raise the hearts of your hearers to a just and high esteem of this gospel of grace, and impress them with an awful sense of the divine importance and worth of it, be not afraid to lay human nature low, and to represent it in its ruins by the fall of the first Adam. It is the vain exaltation of ruined nature, that makes the gospel so much despised in our age. Labour, therefore, to make them see and feel the deplorable state of mankind as described in scripture, that by one man sin entered into the world, and death by sin, and a sentence of death hath passed upon all men, for that all have sinned; let them hear and know that Jews and gentiles are all under sin, that there is none righteous, no, not one; that every mouth may be stopped, and all the world may appear guilty before God. Let them know that it is not in man that walketh to direct his steps; that we are not sufficient of ourselves to think any good thing; that we are without strength, alienated from the life of God through the ignorance and darkness of our understandings, and are by nature children of disobedience, and children of wrath; that we are unable to recover ourselves out of these depths of wretchedness without the condescensions of divine grace, and that the gospel of Christ is introduced as the only sovereign remedy and relief under all this desolation of nature, this overwhelming distress, neither is there salvation in any other, for there is none other name under heaven given among men, whereby we must be saved; Acts iv. 12. And they that wilfully and obstinately reject this message of divine love, must perish without remedy and without hope; for there remains no more sacrifice for sin, but a certain fearful expectation of vengeance; Heb. x. 26. By this conduct you will approve yourself to be a faithful messenger of Christ in good earnest, a minister of the New Testament, and a workman that needs not to be ashamed, if you take special seasons to discover to men what the word of God reveals concerning their misery, and declare to them the whole counsel of God for their salvation, I entreat you, my dear friend and brother, to get it deeply impressed on your heart, that as (I believe) your real and sincere design is to save the souls of men from sin and eternal death, so it is the gospel of Christ which is the only instrument whereby you can ever hope to attain this blessed end; and that for two reasons.

1. It is this gospel, which, in its own nature, is most happily suited in all the parts of it to this great design; and no other schemes which the wit or reason of man can contrive are so: It is the voice of pardoning grace and reconciliation to God by Jesus Christ, that powerfully allures and encourages the awakened sinner, to return to his duty to God and his Maker: It is the promise of divine assistance to enable us to mortify sin, and to practice holiness, which animates the feeble creature to attempt it: It is the attractive view of heavenly blessedness as revealed in the gospel, that invites the soul onward to make its way through all the dangerous enticements and terrors of this world, which is at enmity with God. The divine fitness of this gospel of grace, to restore fallen man to the favour and image of his Maker, is so various and astonishing, that to describe it in all instances would require a large volume.

And 2. As the gospel is so happily suited to attain these ends, so it is the only effectual means that God has appointed, in the lips of his ministers, for this purpose. It is with these wondrous discoveries of this gospel, that he furnished the minds and lips of the fishermen and illiterate persons, when he sent them forth to convert and save a perishing world. These were the sacred weapons with which they were armed, when our exalted Saviour gave them commission to travel through the dominions of Satan, which were spread over the heathen countries, and to raise up a kingdom for himself amongst them. It was with principles, rules, and motives, derived from this gospel, that they were sent to attack the reigning vices of mankind, to reform profligate nations, and to turn them from dumb idols to serve the living God. And though St. Paul were a man of learning above the rest, yet he was not sent to preach the enticing words of man's wisdom, nor to talk as the disputers of the age and philosophers did in their schools; but his business was to preach Christ crucified: Though this doctrine of the cross and the Son of God hanging upon it, was a stumbling block to the Jews, and the Greeks counted it foolishness, yet to them that were called, both Jews and Greeks, this doctrine was the power of God, and the wisdom of God for the salvation of men. And therefore St. Paul determined to know nothing among them, in comparison of the doctrine of Christ and him crucified. These were the weapons of his warfare, which were mighty through God to the pulling down of the strongholds of sin and Satan in the hearts of men, and brought every thought into captivity to the obedience of Christ.

Had you all the refined science of Plato or Socrates, all the skill in morals that ever was attained by Zeno, Seneca or Epictetus; were you furnished with all the flowing oratory of Cicero, or the thunder of Demosthenes; were all these talents and excellencies united in one man, and you were the person so richly endowed, and could you employ them all in every sermon you preach, yet you could have no reasonable hope to convert and save one soul in Great Britain, where the gospel is puplished, while you lay aside the glorious gospel of Christ, and leave it entirely ous of your discouses. Let me proceed yet further and say, had you the fullest acquaintance that ever man acquired with all the principles and duties of natural religion, both in its regard to God and to your fellow-creatures, had you the skill and tongue of an angel to range all these in their fairest order, to place them in their fullest light, and to pronounce and represent the whole law of God with such force and splendour to a British auditory as was done to the Israelites, at Mount Sinai, you might perhaps lay the consciences of men under deep conviction, for by the law is the knowledge of sin: But I am fully persuaded you would never reconcile one soul to God, you would never change the heart of one sinner, nor bring him into the favour of God, nor fit him for the joys of heaven, without this blessed gospel which is committed to your hands.

The great and glorious God is jealous of his own authority, and of the honour of his Son Jesus; nor will he condescend to bless any other methods for obtaining so divine an end, than what he himself has prescribed; nor will his Holy Spirit, whose office is to glorify Christ, stoop to concur with any other sort of means for the saving of sinners, where the name and offices of his Son, the only appointed Saviour, are known, and despised and neglected. It is the gospel alone that is the power of God to salvation. If the prophets will not stand in his counsel, nor cause the people to hear his words, they will never be able to turn Israel from the iniquity of their ways, nor the evil of their doings; Jer. xxiii. 22.

Is it so seasonable a practice in this age, to neglect these evangelic themes, and to preach up virtue, without the special principles and motives with which Christ has furnished us, when there are such numbers amongst us who are fond of heathenism, who are endeavouring to introduce it again into a christian country and to spread the poison of infidelity through a nation called by his name? If this be our practice, our hearers will begin to think indeed that infidels may have some reason on their side, and that the glorious doctrines of the gospel of Christ are not so necessary as our fathers, thought them, while they find no mention of them in the pulpit, no use of them in our discourses from week to week, and from month to month, and yet we profess to preach for the salvation of souls. Will this be our glory to imitate the heathen philosophers, and to drop the gospel of the Son of God? To be complimented by unbelievers as men of superior sense, and as deep reasoners, while we abandon the faith of Jesus, and starve the souls of our hearers, by neglecting to distribute to them this bread of life, which came down from heaven? O let us who are his ministers remember the last words of our departing Lord, Go, preach the gospel to every nation: He that believeth and is baptized shall be saved; and he that believeth not shall be damned; and lo, I am with you alway, to the end of the world; Mark xvi. 15, 16. Matt. xxviii. 20. Let us fulfil the command, let us publish the threatening with the promise, and let us wait for the attendant blessing.

Wheresoever this gospel is published with clear and proper evidence, the belief of it is made necessary to salvation, and it is part of the commission of ministers to make known this to the people; nor is there any thing else which can stand in the room and stead of this gospel, or attain those happy purposes for which this holy institution was designed. Unless, therefore, you have such a high esteem for the gospel of Christ, and such a sense of its divine worth and power, as to take it along with you when you desire to save souls, you had better lay down the ministry and abandon your sacred profession, for you will but spend your strength for nought, and waste your breath in vain declamations: You will neither save your own soul, nor them that hear you; and you will have a terrible account to give at the last day, what you have done with this gospel which was entrusted with you for the salvation of men: You have hid this divine talent in the earth, you have traded entirely with your own stock, you have compassed yourself about with sparks of light of your own kindling, and you must lie down in sorrow with eternal loss. Forgive me, my dear brother and friend, and you, my beloved and honoured brethren in the ministry, forgive me, if I have indulged too much vehemence in this part of my discourse; if I have given too great a loose to pathetic language on this needful subject. I doubt not but your own consciences bear me witness, that this elevated foice is not the voice of reproof, but of friendly warning; and, I persuade myself, that you all join with me in this sentiment, that if ever we are so happy as to reform the lives of our hearers, to convert their hearts to God, and to train them up for heaven, it must be done by the principles of the gospel of Christ. On the occasion of such a head of advice, therefore, I assure myself you will forgive these warm emotions of spirit. Can there be any juster cause or season to exert fervour and zeal, than while we are pleading for the name, and honour, and kingdom of our adored Jesus? Let him live, let him reign for ever on his throne of glory; let him live upon our lips, and reign in all our ministrations.

Thus have I finished my third exhortation relating to the preparation of your sermons for the pulpit.

APPENDIX V

A selection of the most popular 20 of Isaac **Watts's** Psalms and Hymns (all of which are referred to in the text).

1. Psalm 72

Jesus shall reign where'er the sun
Does his successive journeys run;
His kingdom stretch from shore to shore
Till moons shall wax and wane no more.

For him shall endless prayer be made,
And praises throng to crown his head;
His name like sweet perfume shall rise
With ev'ry morning sacrifice.

People and realms of ev'ry tongue
Dwell on his love with sweetest song;
And infant voices shall proclaim
Their early blessings on his name.

Blessings abound where'er he reigns,
The pris'ner leaps to lose his chains;
The weary find eternal rest,
And all the sons of want are bless'd.

2. Psalm 90

Our* God, our help in ages past,
Our hope for years to come,
Our shelter from the stormy blast,
And our eternal home.

Under the shadow of thy throne
Thy saints have dwelt secure;
Sufficient is thine arm alone,
And our defence is sure.

Before the hills in order stood,
Or earth receiv'd her frame,
From everlasting thou art God,
To endless years the same.

A thousand ages in thy sight
Are like an ev'ning gone;
Short as the watch that ends the night
Before the rising sun.

Time, like an ever-rolling stream,
Bears all its sons away,
They fly, forgotten, as a dream
Dies at the op'ning day.

Our God, our help in ages past,
Our hope for years to come,
Be thou our guard while troubles last,
And our eternal home.

3. Psalm 92

Sweet is the work, my God, my King,
To praise thy name, give thanks and sing,
To show thy love by morning light,
And talk of all thy truth at night.

Sweet is the day of sacred rest,
No mortal cares shall seize my breast;
O may my heart in tune be found,
Like David's harp of solemn sound!

My heart shall triumph in my Lord,
And bless his works, and bless his word;
Thy works of grace, how bright they shine!
How deep thy counsels! how divine!

But I shall share a glorious part
When grace hath well refin'd my heart;
And fresh supplies of joy are shed,
Like holy oil, to cheer my head.

Then shall I see, and hear, and know
All I desir'd or wish'd below;
And ev'ry power find sweet employ
In that eternal world of joy.

* Original wording

4. Psalm 117

From all that dwell below the skies
Let the Creator's praise arise;
Let the Redeemer's name be sung
Through ev'ry land, by ev'ry tongue.

Eternal are thy mercies, Lord,
Eternal truth attends thy word;
Thy praise shall sound from shore to shore,
Till suns shall rise and set no more.

5. Psalm 118

This is the day the Lord hath made,
He calls the hours his own;
Let heav'n rejoice, let earth be glad,
And praise surround the throne.

To-day he rose and left the dead,
And Satan's empire fell;
To-day the saints his triumphs spread,
And all his wonders tell.

Hosanna to th'anointed King,
To David's holy Son;
Help us, O Lord; descend and bring
Salvation from thy throne.

Bless'd be the Lord, who comes to men
With messages of grace;
Who comes in God his Father's name
To save our sinful race.

Hosanna in the highest strains
The church on earth can raise;
The highest heav'ns, in which he reigns,
Shall give him nobler praise.

6. Psalm 122

How pleas'd and bless'd was I
To hear the people cry,
"Come, let us seek our God to-day!"
Yes, with a cheerful zeal
We haste to Sion's hill,
And there our vows and honours pay.

Sion, thrice happy place,
Adorn'd with wondrous grace,
And walls of strength embrace thee round;
In thee our tribes appear
To pray, and praise, and hear
The sacred gospel's joyful sound.

There David's greater Son
Has fix'd his royal throne,
He sits for grace and judgment there:
He bids the saint be glad,
He makes the sinner sad,
And humble souls rejoice with fear.

May peace attend thy gate,
And joy within thee wait
To bless the soul of ev'ry guest!
The man that seeks thy peace,
And wishes thine increase,
A thousand blessings on him rest!

My tongue repeats her vows,
"Peace to this sacred house!"
For there my friends and kindred dwell;
And since my glorious God
Makes thee his bless'd abode,
My soul shall ever love thee well.

7. Psalm 136

Give to our God immortal praise;
Mercy and truth are all his ways;
Wonders of grace to God belong,
Repeat his mercies in your song.
Give to the Lord of lords renown,
The King of kings with glory crown:
His mercies ever shall endure,
When lords and kings are known no more.

He built the earth, he spread the sky,
And fix'd the starry lights on high:
Wonders of grace to God belong,
Repeat his mercies in your song.
He saw the Gentiles dead in sin,
And felt his pity work within:
His mercies ever shall endure,
When death and sin shall reign no more.

He sent his Son with power to save
From guilt, and darkness, and the grave:
Wonders of grace to God belong,
Repeat his mercies in your song.
Through this vain world he guides our feet,
And leads us to his heav'nly seat:
His mercies ever shall endure,
When this vain world shall be no more.

8. Psalm 146

I'll praise my Maker with my breath,
And when my voice is lost in death,
Praise shall employ my nobler powers:
My days of praise shall ne'er be past,
While life, and thought, and being last,
Or immortality endures.

Happy the man whose hopes rely
On Israel's God: he made the sky,
And earth, and seas, with all their train:
His truth for ever stands secure;
He saves th'oppress'd, he feeds the poor,
And none shall find his promise vain.

The Lord hath eyes to give the blind;
The Lord supports the sinking mind;
He sends the lab'ring conscience peace;
He helps the stranger in distress,
The widow and the fatherless,
And grants the pris'ner sweet release.

I'll praise him while he lends me breath;
And when my voice is lost in death,
Praise shall employ my nobler powers:
My days of praise shall ne'er be past,
While life, and thought, and being last,
Or immortality endures.

9.

When I survey the wondrous cross
On which the Prince of glory died,
My richest gain I count but loss,
And pour contempt on all my pride.

Forbid it, Lord, that I should boast,
Save in the death of Christ my God!
All the vain things that charm me most,
I sacrifice them to his blood.

See from his head, his hands, his feet,
Sorrow and love flow mingled down!
Did e'er such love and sorrow meet,
Or thorns compose so rich a crown!

Were the whole realm of nature mine,
That were a present far too small;
Love so amazing, so divine,
Demands my soul, my life, my all.

10.

There is a land of pure delight,
Where saints immortal reign;
Infinite day excludes the night,
And pleasures banish pain.

There everlasting spring abides,
And never-withering flowers:
Death, like a narrow sea, divides
This heav'nly land from ours.

Sweet fields beyond the swelling flood
Stand dress'd in living green:
So to the Jews old Canaan stood,
While Jordan roll'd between.

But timorous mortals start and shrink
To cross this narrow sea,
And linger shiv'ring on the brink,
And fear to launch away.

Could we but climb where Moses stood,
And view the landscape o'er,
Not Jordan's stream, nor death's cold flood,
Should fright us from the shore.

11.

We give immortal praise
To God the Father's love,
For all our comforts here,
And better hopes above:
He sent his own
Eternal Son
To die for sins
That man had done.

To God the Son belongs
Immortal glory too,
Who bought us with his blood
From everlasting woe:
And now he lives,
And now he reigns,
And sees the fruit
Of all his pains.

To God the Spirit's name
Immortal worship give,
Whose new-creating power
Makes the dead sinner live:
His work completes
The great design,
And fills the soul
With joy divine.

Almighty God! to thee
Be endless honours done,
The undivided Three,
And the mysterious One:
Where reason fails
With all her powers,
There faith prevails
And love adores.

12.

Come, let us join our cheerful songs
With angels round the throne;
Ten thousand thousand are their tongues,
But all their joys are one.

"Worthy the Lamb that died," they cry,
"To be exalted thus:"
"Worthy the Lamb," our lips reply,
"For he was slain for us".

Jesus is worthy to receive
Honour and power divine;
And blessings more than we can give,
Be, Lord, forever thine.

Let all that dwell above the sky,
And air, and earth, and seas,
Conspire to lift thy glories high,
And speak thine endless praise.

The whole creation join in one,
To bless the sacred name
Of him that sits upon the throne,
And to adore the Lamb.

13.

We are a garden wall'd around,
Chosen and made peculiar ground;
A little spot enclosed by grace
Out of the world's wide wilderness.

Like trees of myrrh and spice we stand,
Planted by God the Father's hand;
And all his springs in Sion flow,
To make the young plantation grow.

Awake, O heav'nly wind! and come,
Blow on this garden of perfume;
Spirit divine! descend and breathe
A gracious gale on plants beneath.

Make our best spices flow abroad,
To entertain our Saviour God;
And faith, and love, and joy appear,
And ev'ry grace be active here.

14.

Are we the soldiers of the cross?
The followers of the Lamb?
And shall we fear to own his cause,
Or blush to speak his name?

Now must we fight if we would reign:
Increase our courage, Lord!
We'll bear the toil, endure the pain,
Supported by thy word.

Thy saints in all this glorious war
Shall conquer, though they're slain:
They see the triumph from afar,
And shall with Jesus reign.

When that illustrious day shall rise,
And all thy armies shine,
In robes of vict'ry through the skies,
The glory shall be thine.

15.

Behold the glories of the Lamb
Amidst his Father's throne;
Prepare new honours for his name,
And songs before unknown. ....

Let elders worship at his feet,
The church adore around,
With vials full of odours sweet,
And harps of sweeter sound.

Those are the prayers of the saints,
And these the hymns they raise,
Jesus is kind to our complaints,
He loves to hear our praise.

Now to the Lamb that once was slain
Be endless blessings paid;
Salvation, glory, joy remains
Forever on thy head.

Thou hast redeem'd our souls with blood,
Hast set the pris'ners free;
Hast made us kings and priests to God,
And we shall reign with thee.

The worlds of nature and of grace
Are put beneath thy power;
Then shorten these delaying days,
And bring the promis'd hour.

16.

Awake, our souls; away, our fears,
Let ev'ry trembling thought begone;
Awake, and run the heav'nly race,
And put a cheerful courage on.

True, 'tis a strait and thorny road,
And mortal spirits tire and faint;
But they forget the mighty God,
That feeds the strength of ev'ry saint.

Thee, mighty God! whose matchless power
Is ever new and ever young,
And firm endures, while endless years
Their everlasting circles run.

From thee, the overflowing spring,
Our souls shall drink a fresh supply,
While such as trust their native strength
Shall melt away, and droop, and die.

Swift as an eagle cuts the air,
We'll mount aloft to thine abode;
On wings of love our souls shall fly,
Nor tire amidst the heav'nly road.

17.

How beauteous are their feet
Who stand on Sion's hill!
Who bring salvation on their tongues,
And words of peace reveal!

How charming is their voice!
How sweet the tidings are!
"Sion, behold thy Saviour King;
He reigns and triumphs here."

How happy are our ears
That hear this joyful sound,
Which kings and prophets waited for,
And sought, but never found!

How blessed are our eyes
That see this heav'nly light!
Prophets and kings desir'd it long,
But died without the sight.

The Lord makes bare his arm
Through all the earth abroad;
Let ev'ry nation now behold
Their Saviour and their God!

18.

Come, we that love the Lord,
And let our joys be known;
Join in a song with sweet accord,
And thus surround the throne.

The sorrows of the mind
Be banish'd from the place;
Religion never was design'd
To make our pleasures less.

Let those refuse to sing
That never knew our God;
But fav'rites of the heav'nly King
May speak their joys abroad.

The hill of Sion yields
A thousand sacred sweets,
Before we reach the heav'nly fields,
Or walk the golden streets.

Then let our songs abound,
And ev'ry tear be dry;
We're marching thro' Immanuel's ground
To fairer worlds on high.

19.

I'm not asham'd to own my Lord,
Or to defend his cause;
Maintain the honour of his word,
The glory of his cross.

Jesus, my God! I know his name,
His name is all my trust;
Nor will he put my soul to shame,
Nor let my hope be lost.

Firm as his throne his promise stands,
And he can well secure
What I've committed to his hands
Till the decisive hour.

Then will he own my worthless name
Before his Father's face,
And in the new Jerusalem
Appoint my soul a place.

20.

Alas! and did my Saviour bleed?
And did my Sov'reign die?
Would he devote that sacred head
For such a worm as I?

Was it for crimes that I had done
He groan'd upon the tree?
Amazing pity! grace unknown!
And love beyond degree!

Well might the sun in darkness hide,
And shut his glories in,
When God, the mighty Maker, died
For man, the creature's sin.

Thus might I hide my blushing face,
While his dear cross appears;
Dissolve my heart in thankfulness,
And melt my eyes to tears,

But drops of grief can ne'er repay
The debt of love I owe;
Here, Lord, I give myself away;
'Tis all that I can do.

Southampton in the 17th Century

Below is an Index to the Map on the back cover:

A	Water Gate	Z	The Castle.
B	Custom house	3	Castle lane
C	Gods house	4	Castle Gate
D	Gods house gate	5	Barr Gate
E	Gods house grene	6	English stret
F	The Friers	7	East stret
G	The Friers Rum	8	Broker lane
H	S Iohns church	9	East Gate
I	Brod Lane	10	Alhallowes
K	French strete	11	Alhal without
L	West Gate	12	Canshut lane
M	Bull stret	13	The Butts
N	Bull hall	14	Beyond yͤ wale
O	West Hall	15	Bargreive
P	West Key	16	S. Mary stret
Q	Lords lane	17	Orchard lane
R	Fish market	18	S. Maryes
S	S. Michaels	19	The Chantree
T	Holy Rode	20	Salt Marshe
V	S. Laurence	21	Cross house
W	New Corner	22	Ytching Ferry
Y	Simnel stret	23	Admiralty
X	Biddles Gate		Gallows